TRUTH IS
A PATHLESS LAND

TRUTH IS
A
PATHLESS LAND

A Journey with KRISHNAMURTI

Ingram Smith

*This publication made possible with
the assistance of the Kern Foundation*

**The Theosophical Publishing House
Wheaton, Ill. U.S.A.
Madras, India/London, England**

©1989 by Ingram Smith
A Quest original. First Edition 1989

The Theosophical Publishing House
306 West Geneva Road
Wheaton, IL 60187

A publication of the Theosophical Publishing House, a department of the Theosophical Society in America.

Library of Congress Cataloging-in-Publication Data

Smith, Ingram.
   Truth is a pathless land.

   (A Quest original)
   1. Krishnamurti, J. (Jiddu), 1895-1986   . I. Title.
B5134.K754S65   1989   181'.4   88-40487
ISBN 0-8356-0643-0

Printed in the United States of America

Cover art by Madhu

I was once the head of a world-wide organization founded in 1911 with thousands of members in many countries. It was dissolved by me in 1929. I said then that there was no path to truth and that no organization or organized belief as religion can lead man to truth or his salvation. I said then that in all so-called spiritual matters there is no authority, no leader or guru, and that all following perverts the follower. You have to be your own teacher and your own disciple.

After all these years I still maintain this essential truth. Following blindly or according to pleasure or temperament does not bring man to freedom. And without freedom there is no truth. In all these many years of talks and dialogues this has been the principal concern.

J. Krishnamurti, Report of a
meeting of the Krishnamurti
Foundations, July 10, 1973

Table of Contents

Acknowledgments

Thanks to the Krishnamurti Foundation of America for permission to quote from the following:

Pamphlet "J. Krishnamurti," from which the introduction was adapted

Krishnamurti's 1947 Madras talk

Krishnamurti's 1929 talk at the Ommen camp.

"A Parable" is quoted from *There Is No Escape*, Ingram Smith, editor, Sydney, McNiven Publishing Guild, 1951, p. 34. The booklet includes contributions by Pupul Jayakar, Gordon Pearce, H. W. Methorst, Richard Weiss, Kim Christen, and others.

Introduction

J. Krishnamurti, 1895-1986

Krishnamurti, at the outset of his life's work over fifty years ago, said that his only concern was to set men and women absolutely, unconditionally free. Until his death in 1986 he traveled throughout the world speaking to audiences on every continent. In support of his work five Foundations were established to coordinate the activities which grew out of his worldwide talks.

In his talks, Krishnamurti asked for a particular kind of participation on the part of the audience. He was not giving a predetermined lecture to which the audience listened with agreement or disagreement; he was not presenting a point of view, doing propaganda for an idea, belief or dogma, or leading the audience to a particular conclusion. Instead the speaker and listeners were together exploring human problems. This is an art that is learned in the very act of attending to what Krishnamurti is saying. This attention is not an effort of concentration; it comes naturally when one is deeply concerned with the many problems of existence.

It is central to Krishnamurti's teaching that for us to be truly free we must first be aware of the psychological conditioning which prevents us from seeing things as they really are. This quality

1

of attention to "what is"—not to what one likes or dislikes, nor to what some authority says is so, but to the actual thing itself—is at the very core of his work. In this attention the mind stops chattering and is still. There is only "what is," and in this there is the quality of love, of beauty, of order.

Krishnamurti was born in May, 1895, in a small town in South India near Madras. As the eighth child of a Brahmin family and a boy, he was by tradition called "Krishnamurti" in honor of Shri Krishna, a Hindu divinity born an eighth child. As a boy he was discovered by C. W. Leadbeater, an eminent Theosophist, and brought to live at Adyar, the international headquarters of the Theosophical Society. There its President, Annie Besant, along with Leadbeater, helped train him for his future role as a Teacher known throughout the world. In 1911 the almost sixteen-year-old Krishnamurti, with his younger brother, was brought to England where he was privately educated. He began to speak along lines that broke with all tradition in 1929, when he repudiated all connections with organized religions and ideology. From then on Krishnamurti traveled the world, writing, speaking, and discussing.

Since he came of age, Krishnamurti never stayed anywhere for more than a few months and did not consider that he belonged to any country, nationality, or culture. He accepted no fees for his talks nor royalties on his books and recordings.

Many years ago he said, "So, if you want to spread these teachings, live them, and by your life you will be spreading them, you will be communicating them, which is more true and significant than verbal repetition, for repetition is imitation and imitation is not creativeness. You as an individual must awake to your own conditioning and thereby free yourself and hence give love to another.'' (Madras talk, December 28, 1947)

A Parable

A man who lived in a small village found his hands were manacled. How he came to be hand-cuffed is of no importance. It may have been a policeman, his wife, the mores of society, his religion, his education; more likely he had unwittingly locked the bracelets on himself. What is important is that he suddenly realized he could not use his hands freely, that he was constricted.

For some time he wrestled with the cuffs and their interlocking chain, hoping to break free. He tried to force the encircling steel rings over his hands. He merely tore the skin, lacerated the flesh.

Defeated and anxious he went out into the streets seeking someone who could release him. Though most offered advice and a few actually tried to free his hands, their efforts always resulted in further bruising, aggravating the pain—and the disappointment and distress. Soon his wrists became so sore he was afraid to ask for help...yet he knew he could not tolerate the constant hurt—and the bondage.

Desperate, he wandered the streets until—as he passed a noisy blacksmith's forge—he noticed the smithy beating a bar of red hot iron into shape.

He paused by the door watching. Maybe this man could. . . .

When the smithy finished the job he looked up, and seeing the manacles said, "Come in, my friend. I can free you." And, at his instruction the distressed man placed a hand on either side of the anvil, exposing the chain.

One blow and the chain snapped, two more blows and the manacles fell apart. His hands were released, and he was free, to walk out into the sun and the open sky, free to do all those things he wanted to do.

It may seem strange that he decided to stay in the blacksmith's forge—in the grime and the noise. Yet he did.

He felt beholden to his liberator. He had a deep feeling of reverence for, and a wanting to serve, the man who had so easily released him. He thought it his mission to stay there and work. He did, and he made a poor assistant.

Free of one set of chains he accepted another more profound, longer lasting bondage, a manacle of the mind.

Yet, he had come seeking freedom.

A Personal Note

In 1947 eight people interested in Krishnamurti began meeting regularly at my parents' home in Newport Beach, Sydney, Australia, where we read passages from his books and discussed the teachings. They were all-day meetings, on the first Sunday of the month. We all brought our own lunch; tea and fruit juices were provided. The intensity and seriousness grew, as did the numbers (to thirty, and sometimes more).

Early in 1949 came the news that Krishnamurti was to give talks in Colombo, Sri Lanka, in December of that year, and I decided to be there. At that time I was a freelance writer-producer of radio programs for the Australian Broadcasting Commission.*

The decision made, I talked to the Federal Director of Talks, B. H. Molesworth, about a leave of absence, and suggested that while I was in Sri Lanka I could record some programs for the national network. He agreed, and suggested that I also get an in-depth interview with the Prime Minister, D. S. Senanyke, about how Sri Lanka's recent independence was working out. I was happy about the prospect. Letters were written ahead

---

*Since 1984 The Australian Broadcasting *Corporation*.

7

to Senanyke and also to Radio Lanka, seeking permission to use the station's facilities should they be needed. I decided to leave early, so as to have time to acclimatize and to record the programs before Krishnamurti arrived.

When I left Sydney in September, no replies had come. The day before the ship was due in Colombo, I received a cable stating "On arrival please wait in lounge. You will be met. Signed John Lampson, Director General, Radio Lanka." Once the ship dropped anchor, I didn't have long to wait.

Mr. Goonawardner, the man assigned to meet me, was already in the lounge when I entered. His presence assured an easy passage through customs and on to the Galle Face Hotel, where he registered me and saw that I was comfortable. Before leaving he offered to send me a car, if I wanted one. I was delighted with the unexpected V.I.P. treatment, and of course I wanted to see the new, still under-construction-but-already-in-use Radio Lanka station. I did not have to wait until the following day to meet John Lampson. That evening at dinner a waiter handed me a note which read, "Come and have coffee with us." I looked around and Lampson, across the vast dining room, lifted a finger in greeting. John Lampson and his young wife June were charming. What great luck.

The following day the car came at 10 A.M. After I'd seen the radio station, accompanied by Goonawardner, and was having morning tea with Lampson in his sumptuous office, he cleared up the puzzle of this "special treatment."

"I have a proposal for you," he said. "I think we could get on. Would you be willing to take a temporary appointment as the Controller of Programs?'' He explained that he had found himself in a predicament after taking up his appointment as head of Radio Lanka only a month earlier. His administrative experience and abilities as a ranking BBC executive had been impeccable and had won him the post, but he had no broadcasting experience. Now that he was here, the mutually antagonistic Sinhalese and Tamil and Burgher producers were frustrating the broadcasting schedules and undermining his authority. He had to have someone he could trust who had practical knowledge of programing and studio production. Would I take the job?

I did, and found myself involved in racial conflicts and intrigues—in working out how one radio station can broadcast in three languages, Sinhalese, Tamil, and English all and have their programs aired in prime time. Right off, it was obvious why a Sri Lankan citizen could not, in those early days of freedom and independence, be trusted to be racially unbiased, which is why an independent Director General and now a ''foreigner'' had been appointed Controller of Programs as a temporary solution. It was in this capacity that I first met Jiddu Krishnamurti.

Krishnamurti with Annie Besan

Colombo,
1949-1950

First Meeting

Colombo, 1949

A meeting between Krishnamurti and me had
been set up so that we could make arrangements
for the two broadcasts he had agreed to do.* It
was already dark when I arrived at Bodhidasa's
house where Krishnamurti was staying.† I was apprehensive as I waited in the drawing room. I was
about to meet the man whose teachings had already turned my life around, the human being I
most revered, a transformed man, a free man, a
God-like being. Moments later, I was introduced
to a highly nervous, agitated person. The serene
being I had expected was not present.

Most of what happened in the next half-hour is
a confused blur. I remember Bodhidasa introduc-
ing us and leaving; there was a fumbling, unsure
hand-clasping. There were some quick remarks
about the scripts, and Krishnamurti excitedly
picked up a sheaf of typed papers from a table
and began shuffling them about.

---

*These two talks were published in 1950 as *Action and
Relationship*. The talks were broadcast on December
28, 1949, and January 2, 1950.
†Bodhidasa is a Colombo merchant and member of the
Sri Lanka Krishnamurti Committee.

"Here are the two scripts. I wonder if they are too long," he burst out. In passing them over we managed to drop them. They scattered across the floor. We began picking up the sheets and sorting them according to page numbers. As I offered him the ones I had gathered, he gestured to me to keep them and handed me his pile while again asking anxiously, "Are the scripts too long?"

I remember for one detached moment feeling, "This is madness." How could I possibly answer? I had not the least idea how many pages there were, nor any notion as to how fast he would read. Bewildered, I began counting the pages. "Both seem to be too long," I said. "A little too long."

I was in no state to give any accurate estimation of time. I riffled through the pages. There seemed to be too many for two quarter-hour broadcasts. However, I said, "No worry, sir, we can record both programs and do any needed editing later."

"Why not *before* the recordings are made?"

I had no answer and no intention of attempting one then. "Are there any carbon copies?" I asked. He looked bewildered. I recall there was some talk as to when it would suit Krishnamurti to record. When, in great bewilderment, I departed, it had been decided that with the windows open, the acoustics would be adequate, and that a recording van would come to the house at eleven o'clock the following morning.

That arranged, I walked away in turmoil. I had come by taxi, but now all I wanted was to continue walking. I hurried off into the night in the direction of the Galle Face Hotel. There are many lakes and waterways in and around Colombo, and presently I found I was pacing alongside a sheet of water.

What had happened? Every anticipation had been shattered. The serene, poised, liberated master had turned out to be a highly nervous, excitable human being. I was disoriented.

Suddenly it hit me. It was as though I had walked slap-bang into a tree or a wall. The shock of realization stopped all motion. I stood stock-still. The man I had just met was not Krishnamurti, but me. For the first time in my life I had met myself—seen myself, uncovered, reflected in another human being. That overwrought man in the room had been me. It was a devastating realization. I saw that when I am angry, the object of my anger is seen either as the angry person or as the cause of my anger.

With Krishnaji there had been no sense of separation. He had not acted differently from me. I had seen him fumbling and nervous. How insane to have expected Krishnamurti to match my anticipated picture of him; and I understood too the madness of foreseeing *a free man* who would exhibit the qualities I had imagined a liberated human being would have—serenity, God-like authority, detachment. I had met no such entity. There is no such person. I had encountered myself in action, seen a clear reflection, heard my echo in the finely tuned body-being named Krishnamurti. Since then, of course, there have been many occasions when I have been distraught, but never again has there been such a clear mirroring of my confusion.

It took me more than two hours to find my way back to the Galle Face Hotel.

Both talks were recorded the following morning. Both were too long to fit the quarter-hour time slot. They were both given extended time, broadcast in toto, and later published.

The Evening Walks

A few days after that first encounter, Gordon
Pearce rang to ask if I would be free to accompany
Krishnamurti on his walk that afternoon.* I was
delighted to have been asked, little knowing that
the opportunity had come about because Krishnamurti liked to walk fast (at least four miles an
hour as it turned out), and the Ceylonese committee members were not up to such a pace.

My job at Radio Lanka permitted great freedom,
so I arrived at Bodhidasa's house at 4:30 P.M. Almost immediately Krishnaji came out, and with
Bodhidasa at the wheel and Dr. Adikaram in the
front seat, we drove beyond the city to the villages and paddy fields flanking both sides of the
road.† The car stopped, Krishnamurti got out, and

---

*Gordon Pearce was a schoolteacher and tutor to the
children of Maharajas. Introduced "The Scouts" movement to India. Was secretary to the Sri Lanka Education Department. In 1950 he became the principal of
the Rishi Valley School, and later the principal of the
Blue Mountains School at Ootacamund.

†Until Krishnamurti's death in 1986, Dr. Adikaram was
his representative in Sri Lanka. Initiator of Krishnamurti movement in Sri Lanka. Traveled the island talking
to small groups in towns and villages. Chancellor of a
Colombo university since the 1970s.

Adikaram said, "We'll be here when you return."
We set off at a brisk clip.

Not a word was said. Everything seemed miraculously alive. I was highly aware of every movement, of the sky, of the swift flight of parrots as they swept overhead, the patches of jungle, the waving green rice, and particularly of Krishnamurti.

Sometime after five o'clock a stream of buses, overloaded with office workers, came roaring past us. I was intrigued to notice that as each bus approached from behind, Krishnaji reacted in a different way. Sometimes he would walk right on and the bus would go around him; at other times he would quickly cross to the other side of the road; occasionally he would leap over the irrigation ditch running between the road and the rice paddy and walk there while the bus went by. With no two buses did he react in the same way. There seemed to be no habit pattern whatsoever.

As I watched, I realized that in some extraordinary way he was responding to the attitude of each bus driver. He stepped aside for the aggressive driver, and let the accommodating driver adapt his driving to us. He seemed to move in relation to the intention of the man behind the wheel, to be an integral part of the whole movement, of the subtle interplay. Yet each was doing exactly what he intended: Krishnaji walking briskly for an hour, and the bus drivers reaching their destinations in whatever way they chose to drive. It didn't matter to Krishnaji whether he was walking on the road or off it—it was the exercise, the oxygenation of the blood, the freedom of body movement that mattered.

A flock of screeching parrots rocketed across the

road directly in front of us. Krishnaji's reaction was instantaneous and dramatic. He physically shuddered as though the birds had flown through him, then continued on as if nothing untoward had happened.

Our speed in this slow-moving island made us objects of whimsical interest. Villagers stood and watched us as we strode by. Occasionally, as we paced through a village, a pariah dog would burst out snarling or barking. Krishnaji responded differently to each dog. As one approached he would shout, "Get back"; to another he would call softly and let it run alongside him, even patting it. Sometimes children would race up beside us. From one he would distance himself, another he would permit to jog for a while at his side or between us. Again, different responses, always patternless, his action relating completely to the present situation. It was a tremendous learning experience to observe such freedom from habitual reactions.

So began our evening walks. For the next month we were driven to a different location each night and then walked for an hour, except on those nights when there was to be a talk.

One evening Dr. Adikaram accompanied us. He wanted to discuss the possibility of travelling through Sri Lanka and talking to people in villages, towns, and bazaars; of discussing the teachings with them, probing into the domain of self-understanding as well as into their personal problems. Krishnaji asked, "Your financial situation is such that you can do this?"

"With care, yes." And Dr. Adikaram went on to explain that his scientific writing was now earning him sufficient income to live by.

"Then do it, sir."

It was the complete affirmation and confirmation Adikaram was seeking. Profound changes were in the air and were about to become realities through the coming years, not only for Dr. Adikaram, but for Sri Lanka and beyond.

We had stopped. As we began to walk again, Krishnaji asked, "What is the Sanskrit word for 'awareness'?"

Adikaram pondered a moment. "There are a number of words which carry the sense of *wakefulness,* of being alert. *Vijnapitah* is one. *Jnana* is another. Then there's *Janati* or *Jagarah,* or even *Prajna.*"

"They are well-known words among Sanskrit scholars?"

"And laymen, too."

"Don't use a Sanskrit word."

Again Adikaram halted. Krishnaji turned. "To use it is to bring to mind the ancient tradition and to sanction past comprehension. A Sanskrit word will attach what you are saying to the remembered texts. Tell it in your own way, in your own words, what you are seeing. Use modern Sinhalese words."

One evening a few weeks later, as we walked, a question surfaced that had been building up in my mind and was now about to explode. I took a deep breath, but before I had uttered a word, Krishnaji lightly touched my hand, saying, "Not now, sir."

Denied expression, the pressure welling up inside me was held. There was no sense of frustration on my part, only a wonder at what was happening. It was as though the impetus had released itself inwardly. Immediately I felt a

tremendous sense of lightness. Even the question
that had been troubling me had vanished.

One evening Gordon Pearce came with us in the
car. He had known Krishnaji from boyhood; indeed, ever since his uniqueness had been discovered, and he had lived in the Theosophical
Society headquarters at Adyar. Pearce was in the
front seat during the drive out of town, and there
had been talk about those early days. Then, twist-
ing right around to face Krishnaji in the back seat,
he asked, "During that time with C. W. L.* did
you actually see the master K. H.? Did you ever
talk with Kuthumi?"† I was greatly surprised
when Krishnamurti replied, "Yes, I did." And so
was Gordon Pearce, both of us having heard
Krishnamurti discount Masters and teachers and
gurus. And here he was admitting to an old and
trusted friend that he had actually seen the Master
Kuthumi, a nonphysical being. "Did you actually
talk with him?" Gordon asked. "Yes," he answered, "sometimes during the early morning
meditation."

Krishnaji went on to say that under Leadbeater's
direction he rose at four o'clock in the traditional
manner and meditated, and that sometimes Kuthumi was present and a conversation took place.
Then one morning just after sunrise—Krishnamurti was seated in the lotus posture facing
east—Kuthumi appeared in the doorway. Until

---

*C. W. Leadbeater, a leading Theosophist and a bishop
in the Liberal Catholic Church. He discovered Krishnamurti in 1909 on the beach in front of the Theosophical Society headquarters at Adyar, a suburb of Madras.
†Also spelled Koot Hoomi. He was said to be one of
the Masters behind the formation of the Theosophical
Society in 1875.

that day, talking with K. H. had been enough. "That day I wanted more than talk. I wanted not only to feel his presence, hear his voice, but to actually touch him, to make sensual contact. Until that day he had been a voice, a presence standing in the doorway. It was a morning when the sun came clear into the room. Kuthumi was standing with his back to the light. I got up, walked to him and *through* him. I turned. There was no one there. He had disappeared. There was nothing there. And. . .I did not ever see him again."

Sometimes, after we had walked briskly for half an hour or more and we were feeling the exhilaration of movement, we would run for quite some distance. Krishnaji ran with the long easy strides of a trained athlete. When I asked him about his running, he said that back in 1924 Dr. Annie Besant had arranged for him to work out with the American Olympic track team during their training sessions on Staten Island, New York, just before they left for the games in Paris.* This expert coaching, along with Krishnaji's natural coordination and grace, no doubt helped him to run with such rhythm, balance, and style.

This information emboldened me to ask about his walking. Anyone who has ever seen him walk will have noticed his erectness and poise. Did he ever have any instruction in how to walk? "Oh yes."

In the 1930s in Italy he had spent time with the army officer in charge of the training of the Italian Alpine troops in skiing and walking quickly over

---

*Annie Besant was President of the Theosophical Society, 1907-33, until her death. She remained faithful to Krishnamurti.

long distances in snow. He had been shown how
to conserve energy, the whole body moving in
one poised forward flow, the arms swinging loose-
ly from the shoulders, as easily as coat sleeves
from a coat hanger. Even in his ninety-first year,
Krishnaji still walked in this free, austere, poised
way. He walked as he did everything else, with
attentive, highly aware precision.

The first evening we ran, Krishnaji began to
wheeze distressingly. There was phlegm in his
throat. I asked if we should stop. His answer surprised me. "No, sir, I'll run till it breaks." An
idea flicked through me. For a will-less man, this
sounded like a most willful declaration.

We continued to run, he choking, obviously
having great difficulty in breathing. A hundred
yards on, up came a great globule of mucus. Once
rid of it he smiled. "That's it! I had this cold in
Switzerland and now it's gone. Shall we run?"
And off he went again.

I knew then that it had not been "will" but a
sense that the condition was about to break, and
he had assisted its release. An intelligent act,
nothing more.

The Colombo Commonwealth Conference

It was already dark when, one Friday evening after the hour's walk, a huge limousine with the parking lights on was waiting outside Bodhidasa's house. As we approached, a tall figure in white emerged and, open-armed, came to greet Krishnaji. The embrace was mutual. While they stood there talking, I wondered who this friend could be. I noticed that the pennant on the front of the Rolls Royce was the Indian flag.

I left and returned to my hotel. The next morning being Saturday, I arrived as usual, just before eight o'clock, to learn that Krishnaji was not there, that a car had called at 7:30 to take him to breakfast with Jawaharlal Nehru, who was in Colombo for the "Colombo Commonwealth Conference—The Colombo Plan." The man I had seen the night before was Krishna Menon, then the Indian Ambassador to the United Nations. Krishnaji did not return until 12:30—a very long breakfast.

During the Sunday evening talk at the town hall in Cinnamon Gardens, Krishnaji spoke of the problems of independence in Sri Lanka, India, and Pakistan, now just two years in operation. He pointed to the need to understand the ongoing implications of Mahatma Gandhi's policy of nonviolence. He talked at length about ideals as non-facts—particularly emphasizing the ideal of non-violence which was being given such political significance at the time.

He went on to say that nationalism inevitably leads to conflict and war. Here he used an interesting analogy. He said that living on the Indian subcontinent could be likened to living in a large room: better for all to be able to move freely around the whole space than to hang a curtain across, or to build a wall dividing it, so that all had to live in a restricted area and everyone had less space.

After the talk I heard one man say, "He claims not to read. He says he doesn't read newspapers. How is it then that he talks as though he knows what's going on in the political world?" I resisted the temptation to tell him where Krishnamurti had spent the previous morning, that Nehru had most likely talked through these very problems. I could also have mentioned that Ernest Bevan, the British Labour Cabinet Minister, ill as he was, had also visited Krishnaji soon after he had arrived in Colombo.

I Am That Man

During these Colombo talks and discussions, a
pattern of operation was developing that would
continue in the ensuing years: talks on the week-
ends and discussions during the week; talks for
the general public, and discussions for those who
wanted to examine certain topics further.

While thousands attended the Sunday talks at
the town hall in Cinnamon Gardens, the discussions attracted only a modest, dedicated three or
four hundred persons. Most squatted on the floor;
a few Europeans and some of the elderly sat on
chairs at the back and along the sides of the hall.

At one Thursday evening discussion there was a
change. The front row of chairs was reserved.
Gordon Pearce told me that arrangements had
been made for a leading member of the opposition
in the Sri Lanka Parliament—Dr. N. M. Perera, a
barrister and a communist recently returned from
a booster course in Moscow—to occupy this vantage position. The other seats were for members of
the shadow cabinet.

What had happened was that the barrister had
seen in Monday morning's paper, *The Daily
News*, the full-page report of Krishnamurti's Sunday evening meeting. He had been profoundly im-
pressed by the fact that the town hall had been

packed, and that amplifiers had been placed outside so that those hundreds who couldn't get into
the auditorium could sit on the lawns and hear
the talk. No recent political meeting had been able
to generate such numbers or such extensive newspaper coverage. He had decided that he and his
political colleagues should attend a meeting to see
what was so special about the man and to discover what message he had that evoked such a
magnificent turnout and so much acclaim. So he
rang Gordon Pearce, asked when and where the
next meeting was, and the special arrangements
about seating were made. Just before 5:30 P.M.
eleven parliamentarians arrived and took their
seats. All eyes were on them.

Soon Krishnamurti came in quietly, took up his
position on a low dais, and slowly viewed the
audience. "What would you like to discuss?" he
asked. Everyone waited. Then Dr. Perera stood
up. He said he would like to discuss the structure
of society and social cohesion, and that such a de-
bate must include an understanding of the basic
principles of communism. He talked for some
minutes on the logic of state control as the supreme authority, and the proposition that those
who do the work must directly receive the profits
of their labors.

When no one else proposed a subject or question for discussion, it was clear that this man was
important. Not only did he know it, but every
Ceylonese citizen in the hall recognized him and
the importance of his challenge. Krishnamurti
asked if we wanted to discuss this.

No one spoke, no other subject was proposed. It
was obvious that everyone was interested in hearing what Krishnamurti's reply would be. He
smiled. "Well, let's begin." The barrister, who

had continued to stand, took up his political theme. He spoke at length about the basic tenets of communism, of communal use and ownership of goods and property, and the role of labor. It was a clear exposition of the communist philosophy and dialectic.

When he had finished and sat down, I wondered how Krishnamurti would deal with the proposition that the State was all, and the individual subservient to the all-powerful central authority.

He did not oppose what had been said. When he spoke, it was as though Krishnamurti had left his place on the dais facing the barrister and crossed over to the other's side to view the human condition from the communist's position and through his eyes. There was no sense of confrontation whatsoever, only a mutual probing into the reality behind the rhetoric. As the dialogue developed, it became a penetrating search into how the human mind, conditioned as it is, was to be reconditioned to accept the totalitarian doctrine—whether reeducating the race would solve the problems that beset human beings, no matter where they live or under what social system.

There was mutual investigation into the ways in which the communist philosophy actually operated, and the means by which conflicts were handled. And basically, whether in fact reshaping, repatterning human thinking and behavior freed the individual or the collective from ego, from competition, from conflict. After half an hour or so, Dr. Perera was still claiming the necessity for totalitarian rule, asserting that everyone must go along with the decided policy, and be made to conform.

At this point, Krishnaji drew back. "What happens?'' he asked, ''when I, as an individual, feel I cannot go along with the supreme command's decision? What if I won't conform?''

''We would try to convince you that individual dissent, perhaps valid *before* a decision is taken, cannot be tolerated *after*. All have to participate.''

''You mean obey?''

''Yes.''

''And if I still couldn't or wouldn't agree?''

''We would have to show you the error of your ways.''

''And how would you do that?''

''Persuade you that in practice the philosophy of the state and the law must be upheld at all times and at any cost.''

''And if someone still maintains that some law or regulation is false. What then?''

''We would probably incarcerate him so that he was no longer a disruptive influence.''

With utter simplicity and directness, Krishnaji said, ''I am that man.''

Consternation! Suddenly—total confrontation. An electric charge had entered the room—the very atmosphere was charged.

The lawyer spoke carefully, quietly. ''We would jail you and keep you there as long as was necessary to change your mind. You would be treated as a political prisoner.''

Krishnaji responded, ''There could be others who feel and think as I do. When they discover what has happened to me, their antithesis to your authority may harden. This is what happens, and a reactionary movement has begun.''

Neither Dr. Perera or his colleagues wanted to pursue this dangerously explicit dialogue. Some were now showing nervousness. Krishnaji continued, "I am this man. I refuse to be silenced. I'll talk to anyone who will listen. What do you do with me?" There was no escaping the question.

"Put you away."

"Liquidate me?"

"Probably. You would not be permitted to contaminate others."

"Probably?"

"You would be eliminated."

After a long pause, Krishnamurti said, "And then, sir, you would have made a martyr of me!" There was no way of dodging the implications. "And what then?"

Krishnamurti waited, and then quietly went back through the course of the dialogue. He talked of interrelationship, of the destruction of life for a belief, for some blueprint for the future, for some five-year plan; the destructiveness of ideals and the imposition of formulae on living beings. The need, not for environmental change, important as that is, but for inward transformation. When he finished, the meeting was over. There was really nothing more to be said. We sat in a musing communion. Then Dr. Perera rose and slowly, deliberately, weaved his way through the packed crowd facing Krishnaji. Everyone moved a little to make way for him. He walked right up to Krishnaji, who had now risen and was standing, watching, waiting.

Stepping onto the low dais, the barrister opened his arms and enfolded Krishnaji. They stood there for a few moments, in each other's arms. Then, without a word, he returned to his colleagues and the audience began to move.

The meeting was over.

A Young Dutchman

People were constantly seeking private interviews with Krishnamurti. Every morning a leisurely, intermittent stream would arrive at Bodhidasa's house. Appointments were at half-hour intervals. Most came early. As they arrived on the sunny verandah they were greeted, their names checked against the appointment list, and they waited. Some talked, most remained silent, preparing themselves.

On the morning after the Perera/Krishnamurti dialogue, I happened to have the pleasant task of greeting these people. Shortly after 11 A.M. I noticed four men walking up the path. Some persons without appointments came on the chance of seeing Krishnamurti. I looked again at the book. The next appointment was a lady whom I knew by sight. As they approached, I recognized Dr. Perera accompanied by three of his party from the previous evening. He introduced himself and his friends, and then explained that he had rung Gordon Pearce, and that the lady with the 11:30 appointment had graciously relinquished her time so that he could talk with Krishnamurti.

While we sat waiting, the barrister talked about the previous evening. He said he had not expected he would meet a man like Krishnamurti.

He said that before the dialogue, he would never have imagined that a man could be publicly stripped of his social philosophy, have his private thoughts exposed to public view, and remain un-shattered. Indeed, he had felt so well after the discussion that he had decided to see if he could arrange a meeting, and here he was, with three members of the shadow cabinet, ready to go into the whole question of the individual and society with Mr. Krishnamurti.

After their interview, they went quietly out to their car. I had no idea whether their expectations had been fulfilled. However, in a few days I was to learn of a quite surprising outcome. Bodhidasa's house stood beside a main road, and the noise from the traffic had disturbed Krishnaji. Some days later, he was invited to stay at the home of Dr. Perera—and he did.

Another day, a young Dutchman with a flaming red beard and hair came for his appointment, and while he was waiting we talked. I had seen him at the meetings, and we were on nodding terms. He, too, confided his story.

As a young man he had been a Catholic priest in Holland. As his English was excellent, he had been appointed to the Catholic Dutch community in London. Basic religious questions which his superiors had not been able to answer to his satisfaction continued to trouble him. He became increasingly disillusioned with some of the doctrines, and the imposed disciplines grew burdensome. A crisis developed, and he had "resigned" from the church. Instead of going home to Holland, he had immediately sailed for India, hoping to find whatever it was he had not been able to uncover in the Roman Catholic faith. His serious quest led him first to Hinduism, then Buddhism. He became a Buddhist monk, and went through the meditative practices. After some years as a monk, he, like Dr. Adikaram before him, had gone to one of Krishnamurti's talks and had walked away to shed his monk's role, along with his yellow robe.

He had come, he said, to discuss the vulnerable state that had followed the extraordinary transformation that had taken place in his life. And he had a problem. Though he'd dreamed and thought about sex, he had never known physical union with a woman. In his new-found freedom, he had within a few months met and married an Indian woman. As we sat there on the verandah, he talked about his problem.

As a Catholic priest, and later a Buddhist monk, he had learned no trade, no skills, had no business experience, no worldly accomplishments. Now he had a wife who was pregnant, and somehow he had to earn a living. What was he to do? What could he do? As a monk, a mendicant, people had given him food, looked after him. Now nobody was sustaining him. He had a major problem. His time to see Krishnaji came, and in he went.

When he came out he was jubilant. He was in no hurry to leave. While we drank a cup of tea, he talked about what had happened. After he had explained his situation, Krishnamurti had asked, "As a training priest, did you learn Latin?"

"Yes."

"Were you good at it?"

"I was. Latin was my favorite subject."

Krishnamurti had then gone on to say that many sons of wealthy families in Sri Lanka wanted to become lawyers, and that Latin was a required subject for a law degree. ''Why don't you let it be known, advertise, that you teach Latin?''

The practicality of the advice had surprised the Dutchman, not only because it was so direct and simple, but because at that time Krishnaji had been pointing out the the practice of law was a profession to be avoided. And now he was privately urging him to assist law students with their careers. Krishnaji then posed a series of questions.

''What is wrong with giving people what they want? Is it for you to decide what they should ask for? When you have what they think they want, who are you to deny it? Why not allow them to find out for themselves that what they want does not bring the fulfilment they are seeking? You will probably find that there are enough budding lawyers wanting to learn Latin for you to be able to make a living.''

The Dutchman shaved his beard, had his flowing hair cut short, and began teaching supplementary Latin to law students. Before Krishnaji left Sri Lanka, he had begun earning a living by tutoring.

A Cry of Pain

One evening, Muriel Payne, an Englishwoman who had been the principal of the Rishi Valley School, joined Krishnaji and me on our walk. She had come to talk, so the pace slowed down to an amble. As we made our way up a long straight incline we found ourselves walking beside a single file of carts homeward bound from the city. They were ancient, cumbersome, thatched carts with large wooden wheels, pulled by two small brahma bulls harnessed on either side of a central pole.

All were proceeding at the same plodding pace, drivers and bulls weary, having left their villages in the early morning. The thirty or forty carts were proceeding up the side of the road. There was no pavement, and we found ourselves pacing alongside one of the carts.

As happens when three people are walking together and talking, we occasionally changed positions. One time Krishnamurti would be between Muriel Payne and me, another she would be in the middle; then Muriel found herself walking right beside a pair of brahma bulls, the driver sitting on the pole between them. It must be mentioned that Muriel could be described as a "tweedy," brogue shoe type of Englishwoman, who loved animals and would protect them in all

circumstances. When she found herself near the
bull, she noticed the driver kick the animal in the
testicles, causing it to arch its back and lunge forward, jolting its teammate into wakefulness. It's
an age-old technique to urge bulls into action.
Whips and spurs are not used by villagers in Sri
Lanka. A kick by a bare foot suffices.

Witnessing this "brutality" within arm's reach,
she revolted. "Look Krishnaji, stop him! Stop
him!"

Krishnamurti looked—and we continued walking. Our conversation had abruptly stopped. For a
few paces there was silence. Then the driver
kicked the bull again. It grunted and arched
forward.

"Krishnaji, you've got to stop him!" she
demanded.

Krishnamurti's reply was equally dramatic, but
much quieter. "To ease *your* pain?" The implications were vast. A swift high-voltage charge swept
through me and through Muriel.

When disturbed or angry or frightened or upset,
as Muriel was then, the natural reaction is to vent
the pain and the anger onto the object or person
we assume had caused it. Habitually, we deal
with it "out there." It is easier than to admit that
the distress is "in here."

Of course, animals are not to be hurt or
maimed, but tired drivers are unlikely to listen attentively or understandingly to an angry attack.
Usually aggression evokes matching aggression,
multiplying the original problem.

It had been a real learning experience. The implications were to reverberate through me for
many years.

Muriel Payne told me once that on her first

meeting with Krishnamurti, her first appointment, she had not spoken. Not one word. He had indicated a seat. She sat down and suddenly, irrationally, and totally unexpectedly burst into tears and continued crying for the whole half-hour. He handed her a handkerchief and sat through her turmoil with her. When she rose to leave he said, "If you wish, come again." It was the first time in her adult life that she had experienced total, uncontrollable release.

Intuition

When Muriel Payne relinquished the task of ad-
ministering the Rishi Valley School in South India, a new principal had to be found. Gordon
Pearce had agreed to resign from his post as Secretary of the Sri Lankan Education Department.
This meant he would forego his pension. He was
sixty-four at the time, and a government service
pension was paid only if the officer had served
until the statutory age of retirement, sixty-five.
Pearce was willing to take this financial loss. He
was excited about the opportunity to participate
actively in a school where the possibility of
awakening children, rather than conditioning
them, could be developed.

So, during Krishnamurti's Colombo visit and at
his behest, Gordon had provisionally accepted the
post of principal of Rishi Valley School. The questions now were: Who would be the teachers? How
would they be selected? And would the educators
themselves need educating? The location of the
school was a further problem. Rishi Valley, stark
and beautiful and isolated as it is, away in the
mountains of Andhra Pradesh, is 140 miles west
of Madras and 12 miles from the nearest town,
Madanapalle, where Krishnamurti was born. How
to preselect teachers who would be happy there

and so, function well? If for any reason they later turned out not to be satisfactory, real disruption to their lives, as well as to the cohesion of the school, would result.

Hopefully, the elected teachers would be extra-ordinary human beings. Besides their academic qualifications, adaptability, and creativity, a love of children was essential. The candidates had to meet all of the above criteria. If the school was to succeed, a whole range of qualities was needed. It was Gordon Pearce's task during that December/January 1949/50 period, while Krishnaji was present, to choose at least some of the teachers. As an interested outsider, I was invited to take part in these discussions.

Beyond reflecting on the various academic qual-ifications and teaching experience, the task was how to get to know the prospective teacher's atti-tudes and manner.* It was seen to be necessary to invite him into your home to observe how he be-haves, responds to you, your wife and family, to other teachers, and to find out what subjects he likes and dislikes, how he talks, acts, and where his interests lie: a whole host of attributes that make up a human being and would form the basis of relationships. Towards the end of one such dis-cussion, after three possible teachers had shown up, it was decided to invite Krishnaji in to hear what had been done and what was proposed.

Pearce tapped on the door of Krishnamurti's room, which adjoined the drawing room where we were gathered. Krishnamurti immediately joined us, taking a place in the circle on the floor. Pearce gave a resume of our discussion and the

---

*From here on the masculine is used to include both female and male.

situation as he saw it, and asked, "We'd like to know, sir, what you would do to select the right teachers?"

Krishnamurti said, "I am a teacher looking for a job. Interview me." I recall Gordon laughing and saying half seriously, "Will you be? Would you come for a term?"

"No, sir. We are talking about teachers *you* are going to select."

In much greater detail, Pearce explained his proposal. Then Krishnamurti said, "All right. So you would invite me to your home, to your table, and I would be most pleasant to you and your wife and children. I would be on my best behavior. And, if I were as subtle as you are, I would pick up where your interests lay, whether you inclined towards the humanities, languages, mathematics, science, history; and I would go along with your interests. When you took me on a tour of the school, I would be open to whatever you proposed without being sycophantic. In this way I would establish a friendly relationship with you. I would also be playing a role, scheming to impress you."

Gordon responded, "If I sensed you were playing up to me, not being frank, yet I still liked you, I might engage you. But not as a teacher. I could assign you to work on the farm and gardens that supply the school. I would watch you out there, see how you behaved and functioned. If you did a satisfactory job, I could bring you in to teach in the school."

Krishnamurti said, "If I wanted the job and accepted your terms, I would, while I was working in the garden, apply myself not only to the job. I would also be listening for others who felt they were getting a raw deal. I would cultivate anyone who was grumbling about conditions, anyone who was not seeing eye to eye with you. Eventually when you did let me in, I would already have a bond with every dissenter. And if ever I saw you in difficulty, I would, with the aid of that group, challenge and maybe overthrow you." It was an unexpected and startling pragmatic statement.

After a long pause Gordon shrugged. "Then what do I do, sir? Assuming that some one of the young teachers takes teaching at Rishi Valley as a stepping stone to becoming the principal, that he or she is as awake and astute as me, how can I know of this ahead of time? How can I discover here and now *before* he is engaged, before any trouble begins, the teacher's hidden characteristics?"

Krishnamurti said, "Sir, I would do exactly what you have said you will do. I would invite him to table, talk with him. I would take him on a tour of the school. I would do all that you propose. I would be watching, listening to how he spoke, observing how he related to others, how he watched the sky and birds and people. And *particularly*, I would be watching how he looked at women."

Then Krishnaji's voice changed, along with the emphasis. "But. . .I *wouldn't* be watching *him,* how *he* related to people. I *wouldn't* be listening to *him,* how *he* spoke, how *he* watched women, or if it was a woman, how *she* watched men. . .I would be *watching the responses in me* to their actions. I would be aware of my responses, the mirroring of him that was occurring simultaneously in me. On that I would go. On that awareness I would act."

The recruiting of teaching staff for Rishi Valley, 1950, began that morning.

The Exploitable

These were early, heady days and nights. All the world was a challenge.

One morning after a midweek public meeting, I brashly asked Krishnamurti why, on the previous evening, he had allowed so many irrelevant ideas to be introduced. I don't remember what the theme was, but I do remember that the meeting had ended in confusion. He had permitted people to raise questions which were unrelated to the developing direction of the discussion. Krishnamurti's reply was that until a person discovers for himself the futility of trying to think up other angles and new answers to a problem, he keeps the brain churning information. Clarity comes when speculative thinking ceases, for listening is the essential ingredient. Until the limited role of thinking is realized, thought remains trapped in its own confusion. That had happened last night. "You noticed it, so did some others. Confusion stops only when it is seen and dealt with first in yourself. To be told by somebody else you are confused only adds another idea to the existing confusion."

On another occasion I asked, "Why is it you don't actually answer people's questions? Why don't you give specific answers?" He replied, "I answer *the why* of the question. When someone

asks you how old you are, it may not be to discover your age, but to find out whether you are
too old for the job, or too young for the responsibility. Questions are asked in relation to something else. When you ask someone the time of
day, it is related to some activity you have in
mind. Beyond the question—listening reveals the
intent behind the words. Except in physical matters, a specific answer to the specific question is
not relevant. The answer lies in understanding the
question.''

At one early morning discussion the matter of
politicians, political leaders, and dictators was
raised. As ever, Krishnamurti discounted both the
divisions each category implies, and in the ''de-
mocracies,'' the built-in conflicts between government and opposition—the personal power and
egotism that are endemic in all forms of
government.

Someone asked, ''Then, what is the intelligent
thing to do? Everywhere there is the growing
power of the state and politicians and dictators.
Hitler is dead but Stalin is alive, and there is the
new ruler in China, Mao; and nearer to home the
autocratic prime minister. What can be done?''

Krishnamurti's reply was unexpected.

''The dictator, the politician is not the problem.
There will always be those who want power, who
believe they know what to do. It is not the exploiter but the exploitable who needs attention. It
is the gullible, the ones looking for direction, for
guidance, who need examination.

''While you refuse to take responsibility for
your own life and are prepared to let someone
else do your work, dictators will exist.''

43   The Exploitable

For days those words rang through me: "It's not the exploiter but the exploitable who needs attention."

Jokes

On one of the days when I was greeting those
with appointments and ensuring that Krishnamurti was not disturbed, there was a lull. Someone
had not arrived on time. After a while I tapped on
the door, which was slightly ajar. "Come in," he
called. There he was lying on the bed reading a
book. I could see the title, *The World's 2000 Best
Jokes*. I had been told he rarely read, though in
the car on the way to our walk one evening, he
had mentioned Orwell's *1984* and some novels
and essays of D. H. Lawrence. But *The World's
2000 Best Jokes*!!! I was delighted.

Spellbound

During the amazing four months in Sri Lanka—
and particularly from mid-December, 1949,
through January, 1950—the work at Radio Sri
Lanka, the evening walks with Krishnaji, the public talks and discussions, and the small early
morning meetings were to revolutionize my life. I
was under the spell of this extraordinary man. His
depth, his beauty, his otherworldliness, and his
skill in discerning what was actually going on in
those around him and in the world; his clarity,
and the starkness with which he asked direct and
fundamental questions—all this brought my old
way of life to a halt. . .at least for the time being.
I had begun to listen not only to him but to my
own actions and reactions.

Bombay, Paris, Seattle, 1950

Bombay

When Krishnamurti flew from Colombo to Madras, then on to Bombay, I wound up the job with Radio Lanka, took a boat up the west coast of India to Bombay, and arrived there just before the beginning of the talks.

Although the close relationship I had with him in Colombo did not continue, the inward movement that had been occurring within me in Colombo did. Here I was to experience other kinds of discussions, particularly in Pupul Jayakar's home in Malabar Hill.* It was a vast, beautiful dwelling with an enormous drawing room.

One morning near the end of a long session we were all feeling weary from the oppressiveness of the crowded room, and from the heat. It was about eleven o'clock when someone said she was exhausted. "And I have only been listening. You must be tired, Krishnaji?" He looked cool and surprised. "Not at all," he said, "I have not been thinking." Extraordinary! Twenty years later he was often to remark, "I'm doing all the work." Never have I heard him claim to be tired.

---

*Pupul Jayakar was later to become the significant figure and center of the Krishnamurti Foundation in India. Head of the Cottage Industries, etc. Author of *Krishnamurti: A Biography* (Harper & Row, 1986).

Another time when the discussion had come around to the domination thought has assumed over all human activities someone wanted to know how this mental supremacy had come about and asked, "When did it begin?"

"You mean historically?"

"Yes, I suppose so."

"That could lead to speculation. Thought thinking about what might have happened in the distant past. Begin near. Let me ask you a question. Each morning when you waken what do you do?"

"I prepare myself for the day. Beginning with my habitual routine. And I probably give some thought to what I will have to do."

The expression on our faces confirmed a recognition of the common practice.

A woman asked, "What do you do Krishnaji?"

"On waking—before I do anything I ask my body 'How are you this morning?' And my body lets me know how it is, rested, ready to get up and go, or lazy. It shows me any aches and pains. And I listen."

So Krishnaji's day begins with open communion between body and mind. Cooperation. No domination.

Meeting a Beggar

The 1950 Bombay talks were held on the high roof playground of a school at sunset; the discussions were at Malabar Hill, Dongarsay Road. Occasionally a small group met at Mr. Ratansi Naraji's house.*

Krishnaji's attentive "emptiness," his starkness, generated enormous energy and interest. In those days Pupul Jayakar and Maurice Friedman were intensely urgent in their questioning.† One evening we were all seated on the floor in a semicircle facing Krishnaji. Gradually, as the discussion intensified, these two edged their way forward, closer and closer. The theme of the inquiry was dying, and what it is to die. Soon the two were directly confronting him. Their urgency to capture his meaning was so compelling, so stressful that Krishnaji leaned backward, delighted, detached, wholly in control.

"You don't understand. Why don't you get it as

---

*Mr. Ratansi Naraji was at that time working with the Krishnamurti Foundation of India in Bombay.

†Maurice Friedman was a Pole who settled in India in the 1920s. Wrote many penetrating articles about Krishnamurti. Over the years, he was one of the key members of the small discussion groups in Bombay.

51

it is being said, as it is? If I change one word, then you will understand. If I change the word 'death' to 'love,' you will immediately say you understand. You will fit it into your conditioned memory and claim to comprehend. Do see that which *doesn't* fit into the framework of your experience. Truth is always new—never the known.''

During one morning discussion about dependence, a European woman brought up the fact that she always avoided beggars, not knowing what to do when one approached. This raised the whole domain of sympathy and empathy and compassion, and all sorts of basic attributes about giving surfaced. How do you decide to whom to give, and how much? When the beggar is insistent, what do you do? Do you give a coin, an anna or two, a rupee, everything you have? How can you know what the beggar needs? What is there to be done when faced with another's needs?

Now, clearly, if a person asks a simple question like the time of day and I happen to know it, I tell him. We normally answer people in terms of their questions; we give people that which they ask for, or what we think they need. There is always a kind of duality involved in giving, that of the recipient—the one with the begging bowl or with open hands held towards you—and that of the donor ''me,'' giving what is thought to be required. It's all a matter of calculation, of measurement, of separation, and of trying to find out what *I* should do about *their* problems.

It was 11 A.M. when the discussion had finished. Though it was hot, I decided to walk the couple of miles back to the Sea Green Hotel at the far end of Marine Drive. Until this morning, I had avoided beggars, especially the persistent ones who wouldn't give up, like the standard woman with a baby on her hip. Usually I passed by the crippled and the maimed who sat or lay on the pavement, as well. Sometimes I gave an anna or two to get rid of them or to ease my conscience, yet often their persistence angered me, and I had rarely felt compassion when faced with those pleading eyes. I had heard ugly tales about parents who were pleased when a child was born crippled or deformed, since he could become a money earner for the whole family. I had been told stories of organizations that meticulously controlled the districts, the streets, and the locations where a particular cripple or beggar was permitted to operate, for a fee. The entrances to the great hotels and the extensive shopping centers commanded high tribute for the mendacious organizers of begging in Bombay. Whether these reports were true or false I did not know.

However, I did know that I had seen an old man with no hands (they were probably eaten away by leprosy), festering wrist stumps held out—not to receive, but for inspection; and a cripple who walked on his hands, his legs grotesquely twisted behind his back, his feet interlocked to hold them in place. I had seen these human beings. Sometimes I had been deeply moved, often annoyed, but usually indifferent as a form of self-protection.

This morning I was about to experience what I had been avoiding: direct contact. I had to meet a beggar, and it had to be the very next beggar I saw, otherwise I might instinctively select one I could feel relatively comfortable with. The enor-

mity of what I was about to do was daunting—to
meet and greet the first beggar I sighted and let
what happened happen.

I began the long walk up to the Malabar ridge,
over the hill and down the main road to Chowpatty Beach without seeing a beggar. The tide was
out and the stench was terrible. A little way
along, there was a woman sitting on the pavement
with her back to the wall, a small child beside her
and another at the breast. She was surrounded by
red blotches of beetlenut expectoration. I was
probably twenty to thirty feet away when I noticed her. Clearly, she had been watching me for
some time, and as I approached she held out her
hands in supplication, upturned to receive. I
found myself looking into her eyes and she into
mine. I stopped, and the expression in her eyes
changed. Calculation gave way to gentleness and
interest; her hands moved from the receiving position and came together as Christian hands in
prayer, or Indian hands in salutation. I greeted
her the same way.

For a little while we remained there looking in
each other's eyes and marvelling. Then, I was
aware she had taken the baby from her breast and
was holding it out towards me. I took the tiny
black hand in mine. As I did, the little child—
who had been nestling shyly close to her mother,
watching and wanting to be included—leaned forward. I reached out and touched her head. She
gave me her hands.

There we were. I came to realize this beggar
woman was not begging for money, but for love,
for communion—and so was I. Reaching out and
receiving—communion. Her intense eyes were
luminous.

She had no English and I no Marathi. After some timeless minutes I gestured that I would be back. I walked to a nearby hawker of fruit, bought a bunch of bananas and a pawpaw, and returned. The little girl was hungry, and immediately accepted a peeled banana from her mother and began eating. Soon I was on my way. No word had been spoken, nor had there been any exchange of money.

I was to visit the family trio every day. Over the next three weeks a free, quite delightful relationship developed. Always I brought some fruit. Of course, she needed money to live. So do I. Its necessity is one reason why I work. Yet, somehow there was something other in these enchanting exchanges, for me and for her. Money can buy food, clothing, shelter, and amusement, but it could never buy the joy of those meetings. Not money but something beyond, a sense of wholeness, of well-being, of vulnerability...yes, of love....The last time I met the family was the morning before I left Bombay. As I was about to walk away, I offered her some rupees and I saw a querulous look come into her eyes. I suspect that she knew that this was a parting gift.

Clearly whatever I do is done in order to find something beyond, some indescribable...happiness? When the barriers drop, love has a chance.

Fear of what might happen, fear of letting go what I knew or imagined to be true, had prevented me from discovering the freedom there is in meeting fear directly. From then on, I either gave or refrained from giving, as seemed fit in the instance. My skepticism as to beggars' motives and begging techniques was as high as ever, including those of the family trio on the sidewalk at

Chowpatty Beach on Marine Drive. Perhaps it is
not strange that thereafter the approach of a beggar was not to bother me as it had before, nor did
beggars pursue me in the old way. Quite without
effort on my part, a change had occurred.

Speculation as to what would have happened
if. . . if, first up, I had met a streetwise male oper-
ator, is invalid. The fact was, great good fortune
attended that vital first meeting.

A Swift Release

An instance of piercing directly to the heart of a problem, when there is no time for the full story to be told, occurred on the afternoon that Krishnamurti was to leave Bombay and India. A farewell tea party had been arranged at Ratansi's house. Surprisingly, as we were about to leave, Achuyt Patwardhan and Krishnamurti began singing Indian religious songs, harmonizing together and obviously enjoying it.* Others joined in while we half-dozen Westerners listened. Soon after, Krishnamurti asked to be excused, saying he had to complete his packing. We were about to leave when a young man I had noticed at the talks burst in unannounced, asking to see Krishnamurti. Pupul Jayakar took over. "I'm sorry, but you're too late. Mr. Krishnamurti is preparing to leave. You can't see him now." He stood his ground. "I have to see him!"

Krishnamurti appeared at the door. "You want to see me?" he asked gently.

---

*For thirty years Achuyt Patwardhan worked with Krishnamurti at Rajghat, Rishi Valley, Bombay, and elsewhere and is a trustee of the Krishnamurti Foundation of India.

"Yes, urgently." He was almost shouting. "I've got to talk!"

"Come with me."

Bypassing Pupul, the man crossed to Krishna-murti, and as they walked down the long hall towards Krishnamurti's room, we could hear the man relating his problem. Before they reached Krishnamurti's door, we heard the man suddenly begin to laugh. "Ah, yes, of course!" we heard him cry out. Seconds later he reentered the drawing room. He was radiant. "I knew it! I knew he could solve it. Thank you." He glanced around the room, said goodbye, and left. The whole incident could have taken no longer than three minutes. It was a revelation of the immediacy of perception when a person is in crisis, when there is no time for explanations.

Paris

A hall in the rue des 'Ecoles was the venue for
the Paris discussions. There I met Mr. H. W.
Methorst, a Dutchman.*

It was at the first public discussion that Krishnamurti made one of his devastatingly direct ex-
posures of national phobia. He began by talking
about the clarity of the French language, which he
knew well, and the ability of the French to use
words precisely, their pride in articulate speech
and writing, and the fact that the international
diplomatic language is French. After these pleas-
ing opening remarks, he began to demolish the
thinking process, the reliance on words for communication and comprehension, and to point out
that insight is free of words. He went into "consciousness," into what lay beneath the word
"awareness," not the description of awareness,
but the state of being itself. He spoke in English,
sentence by sentence, and paused while a translation into French was given. He pointed out that
thinking in French is no different from thinking
in any language—that pride in the French tongue
engenders arrogance.

---

*With Pupul Jayakar and seven others, H. W. Methorst
was to contribute to a book I later published about this
journey, There Is No Escape, relating to our experi-
ences with Krishnamurti.

Seattle

After the talks, I crossed to London and worked for a month at the BBC. From London I sailed to New York, and went by bus to San Francisco, where I worked in the newly opened NBC television station. In June, Krishnamurti gave a series of talks in Seattle. I flew up the Pacific coast to hear him.

An extraordinary series of revelations was to occur during the Seattle sojourn. An appointment had been arranged to discuss with Krishnamurti the possibility of my doing some work with the editing, compiling, and arranging of the manuscripts of his talks for publication. In those days everything was taken down in shorthand, typed and checked, then prepared for printing—quite a task.

This demanding work was carried out in India by Madhavachari,* and in Europe and America by Rajagopal.† Years later, Madhavachari was to tell me that from 1947 to 1949 (before shorthand re-

---

*Madhavachari was a longtime senior Krishnamurti representative in India. Back in the early 1930s he had helped to establish the school at Rishi Valley.
†Rajagopal was a longtime representative of Krishnamurti Writings, Inc.

cordings of the talks and discussions were made),
he would immediately, after each talk, write down
the whole talk as if he were hearing it again—
much as some musicians are able to listen to a
score once, then go home and play it note for note
on a piano, letting it unravel from memory. Madhavachari said that as he began to transcribe what
he had heard, the whole story would come se-
quentially, sentence after sentence. This is the
way the early post-World War II Indian publications had been prepared. I was concerned that
misinterpretations could occur. I wanted to discover if my radio scripting experience could be
applied to the process of getting Krishnamurti's
talks into publication form.

The first Seattle appointment was for a Saturday
morning at a Professor Will Tyler's house by a
lake, with its tremendous view of Mt. Baker and
the mountains to the east. When I arrived, everyone was preparing for a swim. I was invited to
join in and was given a pair of trunks. The lake
was fairly cold, and I remember that Krishnaji was
timid in the water, and probably could not swim
very well. There were fourteen adults at lunch.

Later, in his room, I put my proposal about
helping with the editing to Krishnaji, and immediately he replied, ''You must see Rajagopal in
Gower Street, Hollywood, and discuss this with
him. There is already talk of a change in the publications.'' He then went on to talk about the
many people who wanted to help. Most offers
came to nothing. He said he had received a letter
the day before, with a check for twenty thousand
dollars from a woman in New York. Although the
money was a gift, he was returning it to her. Apparently it was an attempt to buy her way into a

working association with Krishnamurti. The twenty thousand had not been a *free* gift, but a donation with strings.

Krishnaji was making sure I understood that, should Rajagopal decide to accept my offer, it would need to be free from any personal tags. Krishnaji had read me like an open book. I was willing and wanted to be involved in the work, especially with the publication and presentation of the talks and discussions. Parallel with this new urgency was the feeling that I did not want to lose my independence.

The interview was over, and he had other appointments. I rose to leave. Krishnaji said, "Stay, sir."

Uncertain, I hesitated.

"If you have something else..."

"No, I'd like to stay."

"Then do." He indicated a seat by one of the large windows overlooking the lake, with a view of the mountains.

A middle-aged woman came in. She was distressed and barely noticed my presence. After a while she launched into her complex problem. I heard the discussion almost without listening. When she was through and had left, I was brash enough to ask, "Why was it that you did not go further into her problem? I felt that you didn't go the whole way."

Krishnaji's answer was astonishing. "She came in love. Why go beyond it?" To that there was no answer. He added, "If she wants to go further, decides to probe deeper, she will come again."

It was a salutory lesson. From my earliest observations in Sri Lanka, it had been obvious that probing into the private or undiscovered areas of people's lives is not Krishnaji's way. Only when we ask for another's advice are we likely to listen, and then, being vulnerable, capable of receiving. Only with the mutual consent of both to probe together into the same area of the same problem is free and open examination possible.

Late that afternoon as I was leaving, Krishnamurti walked with me into the garden. As we approached the gate, I began wondering how I would say goodbye—how I could thank him for all he was doing, for the incredible afternoon, for arranging for me to see Rajagopal. Suddenly I realized he was no longer beside me. Turning, I saw that he was already ten yards away. He looked back, waved, and vanished. He had solved my problem of how to say goodbye.

I took a bus down the coast to Hollywood and Rajagopal's house in Gower Street. He met me at the door, barefoot and in his dressing gown.

As we talked, I couldn't help noticing the extraordinary flexibility of his feet and toes. He was rolling his big toe completely under his foot. On occasion I have observed Indian women and children foot-playing in this way, which is quite similar to folding a thumb into the palm of the hand. But never had I seen such pliancy. His feet seemed as flexible as his hands, fingers, and thumbs. If mental subtlety is related to physical suppleness, then Rajagopal indeed has a most lucid mind.

Rajagopal politely let me know that he really did not need help. After all, this was his undertaking, and all was going well.

The next time I saw him was some weeks later at Ayra Vihara in Ojai. We again talked about the work and what needed to be done. I was looking

for something which might give significance to
my life. It was already clear that whatever I might
do, I would have to discover it for myself. I
sensed that while the important outward work
was the spreading of Krishnamurti's teachings
across the world, there was real and immediate
work to be done in freeing the patterns which
constituted "me," and that both tasks were simultaneously possible and practical. Indeed, they
were complementary—freedom in me and in the
world.

The following day I received a cable from B. H.
Molesworth, Federal Director of Talks for the
Australian Broadcasting Commission. The position
of Supervisor of Talks for the State of New South
Wales was vacant, and if I wanted to apply, I
must cable one word, "Yes," right away, and
then send my written application as soon as possible. I cabled "Yes," and very shortly was on a
plane back to Australia.

So ended the first crucial life-changing contacts
with Krishnamurti.

Sydney, 1955

Beneath the Surface

Five years later, in November 1955, Krishnamurti visited Australia for the fourth time, and gave a series of talks. Spencer English, Krishnamurti's representative here since 1939, and I drove out to the airport to meet Krishnamurti and Rajagopal. On the way to Spencer's home on the north side of Sydney Harbor, Raja sat in the front seat with Spencer, who was driving, and I was in the back with Krishnamurti.

As we were crossing the harbor bridge, he asked me, "What would be the proportion of Catholics in Australia?" I didn't know. Every politician and sociologist wants to know the percentages of dedicated Catholics and other ideologically committed people. Any estimate would be guesswork. But he had asked me, and he was expecting an answer. I remembered years ago I had heard that one-third of Australians were Catholics, or of Catholic descent. I told him this. Then he asked about the number of communists. I estimated that one percent were card-carrying members of the party, but that the number of their left-of-center sympathizers, socialists, and others, would be considerable—a third perhaps.

As I was talking, and before we had crossed the long bridge, I realized that, although I had not

known the actual figures and had been hazarding
guesses, I had in a sense answered Krishnamurti's
question. I had been born in the country, was
numbered in the population, and while I had been
speaking he could hear my hesitancies, which indicated what I knew and what I didn't know.
Right then I sensed that in some miraculous way,
I was communicating to Krishnaji what he wanted
to know. There was that extraordinary attentive
listening of his—a stillness. I realized that in
listening openly, the limitations of what is being
said, the hesitation, the falseness, and the certain-
ties are apparent. As I was speaking, I suspected I
was revealing to Krishnaji that which I didn't
even overtly know about myself. After all, I had
grown up in this land, I was inherently a part of
the culture, and I could not help communicating
this. Krishnaji must have been satisfied. After a
moment or two, he was again viewing the water
on that bright morning.

The talks were held at the Sydney Conservatorium of Music. It is a beautiful setting, overlooking
the Botanical Gardens and the harbor. It seats sev-
enteen hundred people, and was crowded for
every talk. One of my jobs was to test the microphones and speaker system, to ensure that Krishnamurti would be heard in every part of the hall
by everyone. Another was to escort him through
the labyrinth of passages and dressing rooms to
the stage when he arrived, and after the talk to accompany him out of the building and to the waiting car.

One evening as Krishnamurti came off the platform, I noticed he was beating his right hand and
arm vigorously against his side and leg. Noticing
my look he said, "My hand's gone to sleep." And

then I recalled that during the talk, he had stood erect and still for an hour and fifteen minutes. Certainly, I had not noticed any movement. An incredible feat, then or at any time. During the next thirty years, he would gesture more.

Another equally astonishing fact was that after each talk, to get to the car, we had to walk along a side corridor and then through the crowded foyer. There was no rear entrance to the conservatorium. Every night en route to the car, I walked a few steps ahead of Krishnamurti to clear a way for him. Only once did someone notice him and attempt to talk. On the other eleven occasions as he walked through, he walked invisibly. No one saw him. It was as though the man had dissolved into nothingness. Certainly he had no persona. That this "absence" was not often perceived is probably due to the fact that on leaving the stage he went out of sight—and, as a presence, "out of mind." He had already gone.

Occasionally, people would remark to me, "I saw you going through the foyer after the talk." They hadn't noticed Krishnamurti, the one they had come to see and to hear.

Odd Experiences

Krishnamurti was staying at Spencer English's house beside the Pymble Golf Course. One day I had an appointment with him, and as I came into the drawing room, Krishnamurti, in his gracious way, indicated an easy chair for me while he sat on an austere stool. That is all I remember. As I began to sit, I recall beginning to cross my legs, and my next recollection was uncrossing my legs and realizing that the appointment was over. I know that sounds quite mad, but it is a fact. What happened in that half-hour I do not know. Amnesia? I doubt it. I walked away feeling light and free.

Another quite astonishing experience happened one morning when we had been talking about freedom. Suddenly I realized I was seeing right through the walls of the house. I could see Barbara English making a bed in a room which I later learned was at the far end of the house, through four layers of brick. As I continued to look, I could see people working outside the house, beyond the furthest wall. There is no rational explanation for this, and I record it simply because it happened.

One night during dinner, there was a violent thunderstorm with lots of lightning—a real No-

vember early summer turbulence in the Southern
Hemisphere. We stopped talking to watch. Krishnamurti pushed back his chair, and without a
word went out onto the open patio and began to
dance in the rain, joyously leaping in the midst of
that extraordinary lightning and thunderous
storm. It was beautiful to watch a man dancing
spontaneously, wildly, and gracefully in nature's
violence.

One day a young man, Bill De Vere, asked if I
could arrange for a number of "YTs"—Young
Theosophists—to have a group appointment with
Krishnamurti. The morning after the meeting, Bill
rang to say excitedly, "An extraordinary thing
happened. For the first time ever, I met myself.
Until yesterday I had seen myself as different. As
we talked, I suddenly realized that in Krishnaji, I
was experiencing a true reflection of myself—a
shattering discovery—to see myself as I am. What
a shock!" There is a singular similarity between
his experience and mine in Colombo.

One evening, Rajagopal and I went for a walk
on the golf links. We again talked of Krishnamurti's books and publishing. I mentioned that I had
given a series of talks in Sydney in 1953, which
had been recorded at the time and later typed.
Picking up my feeling, he asked if I wanted to
publish them. I said I had been contemplating
this. "Let me see them," he said.

When I next went to Pymble, I took the manuscript and left it with him. The following morning, he rang to say he had stayed up very late and
"finished the thing," and that "certainly this
should be published," which it was, within a few
months. The title is *Being What I Am*.

One day we went for a picnic down the South

Coast. Spencer English and Rajagopal were in the front seat, Krishnaji and I in the back. Rather than following the highway, we turned off into the Royal National Park. After we had been driving for half an hour in the virgin bush, Rajagopal said, "This is an enormous park to have so close to the city. How big is it?" I hadn't the faintest idea, nor had Spencer. While we pondered the possible area of the park, Krishnaji said, "One thousand eight hundred fifty hectares." I didn't disbelieve him, but I couldn't help being a little skeptical. "It was on the sign at the entrance gates," he said. This was yet another example of how, for all his inwardness, Krishnamurti never lost touch with the immediate present.

A few days before Krishnamurti was due to leave Australia, Rosalind Rajagopal arrived. Raja went back to California and Rosalind accompanied Krishnamurti on the flight to India for the talks which were to begin that December, 1955.

Mark Edwards

Indian Sojourn,
1963-1978

A Crucial Question

Although from 1955 to 1962, work with the Australian Broadcasting Commission kept me in Australia, I was to have a sequence of Indian sojourns beginning in 1963, which were to go on through 1978. For approximately three months every two years during the winter—from early November through mid-February—I recorded Krishnamurti's talks (1963/64, 1965/66, 1967/68, 1969/70, 1971/72, 1973/74, 1975/76 and 1977/78). Although I had been to India in 1962 covering the Indo-China border war for the ABC, it was 1963 when I first began recording the Krishnamurti talks and discussions.* My first tape-recorded interview with Krishnaji was in Shiva Rao's home in New Delhi.† I had discussed the possibility with Madhava-chari and he arranged the session.

---

*Because of the war, Krishnamurti did not go to India in 1962.
†Shiva Rao is one of the giant gentle figures relating to Krishnaji. It was he who persisted throughout the bureaucratic red tape and delays to finally acquire for Krishnamurti and the Rishi Valley Trust the magnificent Rajghat property. A beautiful being, and husband of Kitty Shiva Rao. While they lived in Delhi, Krishnaji always stayed in their home when talking there.

Before we began, Krishnaji asked me to talk about his Sydney visit back in 1955, thus to establish a relationship and to give a lead into my questions. This I did, and a forty-minute interview followed. As with the half-dozen subsequent recorded interviews, passages were to be broadcast over the ABC network in Australia.

Rajghat, 1963

The day after I arrived at Rajghat,* the Krishnamurti Foundation School near Benares,† an appointment with Krishnamurti was arranged for me. The time and place were five o'clock in the afternoon on the verandah of his house overlooking the Ganges. I came early, and waited in the small gazebo on the high bank overlooking the river. By November, the yearly flooding is subsiding, yet the amazing river is about eight hundred yards wide at Rajghat, four miles east of Varanasi. Many fishing boats seemingly motionless on the water drifted silently, one still figure seated on each stern. Beyond the river, the southern shore was bright green with the new shoots of young rice planted in the mud as the water level dropped. The pale blue sky, the pink cumulus clouds, and the yellow and purple of the coming sunset were reflected in the dark water.

---

*Rajghat School at the confluence of the Ganges and Varuna Rivers. A huge complex, consisting of a Primary School (boarding), Secondary School (boarding), Tertiary College for Young Women (day), plus an Agricultural College. *Raj* = high, royal, great. *Ghat* = Bank, raised land as in Bombay "Ghats."
†Benares or Banaras: the English name for Varanasi. The city lies between two rivers, the Varuna to the east and the Ansi to the west: hence Varanasi.

Entranced, I watched. I was also waiting. So when Krishnamurti lifted the edge of the blind that protected the first floor verandah from the sun and waved, I walked over to the house, up the stairs and out to where he stood. Greetings over, he asked me why I had come. I said I wanted to share the extraordinary freedom and lucidity that came when I was with him, and which I occasionally experienced on my own.

He hesitated. "And you want it? *You* want to get it?" The emphasis on the "you" gave me pause.

"Yes. Even though I realize it's not a personal thing at all, that it's not mine."

He let that go for the moment and we sat in silence. Then I asked about the possibility of breaking through the limitations in my way of life.

"What then is your question?" he asked.

"What is the essence, the free-flowing energy that animates life?"

Krishnamurti's answer: "Energy is always here, but normally it's involved in pursuing thought, is expended in thinking. So that the real world is secondary and your own responses occupy your attention and use up your energy." He was describing my situation. He was again reflecting me, and this was obvious when he added, "When there is no division between you and the world around you, the energy flows freely."

"But," I countered, "Energy in me is confined, is directed, is *not* free."

"And you want to walk free?"

"Yes."

"See through yourself?"

There was a long pause. "Yes."

"It demands tremendous sensitivity."

I was listening intently.

"Are you prepared for *psychological* surgery?"

The dramatic metaphor rocked me. This was no longer a speculative project that I could work on at my leisure; not some transformation that may possibly come about at some future time. It was an ultimate question. Was I ready for the immediate-slicing-through-surgery? No matter what the outcome?

That moment I realized that I was being faced with a total decision: the cutting out of the false. I had no idea what was involved, but I did understand that it meant fundamental change. Was I prepared? Well, ready or not, there I was. There was actually no decision to be made. I had come to this situation and this crisis point.

"That's why I've come," I remember replying.

"Then come tomorrow morning at eight o'clock. When you go downstairs, see Momma (Madhavachari) and tell him that you will be attending the early morning discussions.*

The interview was over. The work was about to begin.

---

*"Momma" is the Hindu word for "uncle."

Early Morning Discussions at Rajghat

The following morning I arrived early once again and wandered around the garden watching the mists on the river and a wild peacock far up in a tamarind tree. Numbers of these exotic birds inhabit the flats adjoining the Varuna River down by the school's playing fields. The school and property lie at the confluence of the Varuna and Ganges Rivers.

I went up the stairs to find eight Indians sitting cross-legged in a circle, five men and three women. They made space and I sat with them. Soon Krishnamurti joined us and straightaway asked what we would like to talk about.

Someone proposed "cooperation," adding "cooperation that has no goal as its motive." Someone else observed that without a purpose there would be no incentive for cooperation—and the discussion had already begun. We went into what it means to cooperate without an objective; simply being together, inquiring together, watching together, was cooperation. The discussion quietly led to the fact that, being conditioned, we project our purposes out of our pasts and so keep moving in the constant round of past-present-future repetitive activity. And that we "cooperate" in this known pattern.

Krishnamurti asked, "Aware that we are this repetitive mechanism, is there awareness that the deadening, recurring process prevents spontaneous cooperation? Maybe there is another movement altogether that is not mechanical, not repetitive?"

The question highlighted the admission that living usually consists of a boring routine, and that, simultaneously, one looks for a way out of the habitual round, to make a passage into another dimension, something new and whole, often called "freedom." Rather than speculate about what freedom may be, simply to observe one's mode of daily living may be the only action needed. Certainly to remain focused on what is actually happening is to uncover its operation (in a thousand ways), and to discover the diminishing significance and power of habit. One of the men pointed out that awareness brings about an enormous release of energy, energy which has been blocked and stored in repetitive patterns.

This discussion group, like the others I was to attend over the years, included a dimension normally beyond ordinary consciousness. It didn't matter what direction our talk took, or what the theme had been at the beginning, for the area being investigated would open out and often change course. As we followed the flow, domains and depths immeasurably beyond the opening understanding were uncovered. There was always a sense of wholeness and urgency. Sometimes during a dialogue, one or two of us would become distressed or troubled. There would be long pauses, followed by a sudden pick-up; baffled responses sometimes erupted. There would be a quick seeing, a quick leaping through one another's perceptions, like a game of mental leap-frog, with each one of us leaping over and beyond the other's stance—no going back to what had been, but a vaulting through the present percep-tion to a new position, and occasionally, into another dimension. I would leave the small dis-cussions with a sense of extraordinary lightness and wholeness.

In the early sixties, these get-togethers were not recorded. Only after the use of the Nagra record-ing machine was there consistent recording.

Drifting Down the Ganges

During this month-long talks-discussion-medita-
tive "seminar" at Rajghat, a new sense of freedom
enlivened my consciousness.

One early evening, two companions and I were
returning from Varanasi where we had spent the
afternoon. We were at the Burning Ghats on the
river bank when the full moon rose, and we decided to hire a boat and drift the mile or so back
to the temple on the school property. Like us, the
boatman was happy merely to drift eastward down
the river under the enormous railroad bridge, just
floating gently on this silent river. Occasionally,
the oar was moved to guide the craft as we flowed
serenely with the silver stream. The night and the
sound of the water lapping gently induced a
dreamlike tranquility, yet we three were starkly
awake.

When we came to the temple steps, which led
down into the water, the craft slid in. We were in
no hurry to move with no wish to change the
magic mood. The boatman was paid, and we
stepped off onto a little stone platform. As though
in a waking dream, we meandered up the steps.

The silence held an extraordinary stillness. No
one spoke. At the top of the bank there was a
giant banyan tree. As I passed under its vast can-

opy, with the moonlight shining through the leaves and making dappled patterns on the sandy earth, a strange sensation came over me. I had a feeling of such lightness and the whole world had suddenly changed—and I with it. Everything was totally different, sharp and clear. It was as if a great burden had fallen away. Everything was right and beautiful just as it was. Perfect.

This sensitivity, fragile yet with wholeness and strength, was to be present through my body-being for four days—a sense of seeing and being in a completely new world. This sounds as though it were a personal experience. It was not. What was happening had nothing to do with me or anything I was doing or had done or intended to do. It was as though my old consciousness was in abeyance. And everything was present and changing its own totality. There was no sense of separation.

In this miraculous state, we walked up to the Pilgrims Way and to our rooms in one of the college residential buildings overlooking the Varuna River.*

---

*Rajghat School, Besant College, and the Agricultural College form a huge and most beautiful campus complex at the confluence of the Varuna and Ganges rivers. A magnificent location which had been the celebrated rest and recreation site for British army officers in Central India until the 1930s—and they chose the best. It was due to the unfailing efforts of Shiva Rao that, after years of negotiation, the property was purchased on behalf of the Rishi Valley Trust for Krishnamurti. The grounds include school buildings, residences, dining halls, a superb auditorium, a post office, an ancient Hindu temple with steps leading to the Ganges, and a Moslem mosque facing the Varuna. Yet this is no iso-

This "experience" was the beginning of wholly tranquil days and nights when the slow rhythm of the daily round, the timeless tempo of the river, the beauty of the dawns and sunsets, the sense of being, and of being timeless, filled the world with wonder.

As I began to come back to my normal consciousness, I jotted down some thoughts.

Perceptions are instantaneous, but although the mood had been there as we drifted timelessly in the moonlight, the change in consciousness had not come until I walked under the banyan tree. At that moment, another dimension was suddenly here. And this raised again the questions: What is consciousness? Where does consciousness begin? Where does it take place? In my brain and head? In my body? Where? And what is it that changes? What actually is consciousness?

When I am introspective I seem to be looking inward to an inner space somewhere behind my eyes. Sometimes I close my eyes not only to listen more acutely, but also to recall something I have forgotten. I close my eyes to *look inside*.

------

lated educational institution. Passing through the property and paralleling the Ganges, dividing the campus, is the Pilgrims Way. Along this ancient path, two thousand five hundred years ago the Buddha walked en route from Sarnath (eight miles away), where he had preached his first sermon after reaching enlightenment," to the sacred city of Bharanasi (Banaras-Benares-Varanasi, the one ancient city). Today, it is a much-used public thoroughfare through the Krishnamurti Schools. In the early morning the villagers take their produce to the Varanasi markets, returning in the evening. And all day people are passing by. Once I saw a string of camels loping along the Pilgrims Way.

Watching this phenomenon I *saw* that closing my eyes cuts out outside distractions, the sights/ sounds of the physical world around me, so that they do not intrude and distract from what is going on inwardly. This introspection apparently behind the eyes indicates that physiologically this is where I assume consciousness is.

When talking, I tend to rely on eye contact as though consciousness were operating in the other's head as well. Somehow I assume that the brain/space inside my head is talking to the brain/ space in some other's head. I imagine mind/space is inside me—in back of my eyes where I cannot ''look''—sight being only forward.

Consciousness can also be feeling butterflies in the stomach, gasping a quick breath, a racing heartbeat. Locating consciousness is an arbitrary role. ''Consciousness'' has no fixed location.

So what is consciousness? Is it simply reactivity to some stimulus?

One thing was certain, an unlocated magnitude was present during those four days.

Letters From Rajghat

November 30, 1963

There is a serene sense of well-being, an inner tingling, a kind of dancing in slow motion. This morning I awoke early, as usual, and walked to the river to watch the predawn colors emerge in the Eastern sky and find their reflection along the vast waterway. As the sun rose, the riverbanks, the trees, the buildings—the whole world—materialized. The very air was penetrated by the light of the sun, as I was penetrated by miraculous light and lightness; the spirit lifted, everything clear. The past days, what I see around me is mirrored in consciousness; what I feel inwardly is out there in the world around me—all one harmonious interflow. This unitary moment, this consciousness of consciousness seems to be the very essence of consciousness.

These words, like all others, are failing to reveal the idle emptiness that is here. Even so, I feel impelled to try to tell you. Impossible as it may be, I urgently want to communicate this wondrousness, to share the silent, powerful joy with you. As I write, every word is a metaphor, a label for something else, a verbal recording, not the living reality. I'm tempted to try to explain by saying ''Well, it is like...." and go on to relate some action or object already known to us both, and thereby hope to communicate something entirely new. Metaphor doesn't actually do the job, and cannot. And there is a further hazard because any metaphor I use to elucidate what I'm trying to convey can only add a different picture. Though consciousness can be shared, it cannot be communicated, and is impossible to translate. Communication is not communion.

Again, I'll still try. At a distance, what else can I do?

These days are filled with a delicious idleness. Two nights ago, a group of musicians played in the auditorium for Krishnamurti, the school staff and students. The subtle drumming on the tablas, the singing, and the plucking of the vina produced an extraordinary atmosphere. As the music developed, I was aware that the rhythm was all through me, a very fine, unmistakable tingling. Every nerve and fiber of my body was alive with the intricate rhythm and the song. As the vibrations moved more completely through me, I became the rhythm, my whole being participated in the jubilance. If I had not been seated there, the sound would have filled the space I occupied—as it was, my body was pulsating with sound, as though I were not there. Separate consciousness, for the time being, had dissolved.

Of course, I didn't think this at the time. I sensed a glorious wholeness and vibrant emptiness. Only later, quietly, consciousness reemerged and "I" was present again. My sense of wonder continued as an afterglow.

Last night, as I walked, everywhere I looked—at the sky, the river, the ancient temple by the

river's edge with the paint peeling from its neg-
lected walls, and across the bamboo bridge over
the Varuna River where villagers were returning
from Varanasi along the Pilgrims Way, and further
on, the village fires, the wheat fields, the groves
of trees—there was a miraculous seeing without
my consciously looking, a learning without intended listening, which lifts the heart and stills
the mind.

It's not strange that all relationships have sharp-
ened and every circumstance is acute and clear. It
is as though time itself has come into crisis—and
stopped. No past, no future, only what is happening is real. All else is illusion, nonfact. All life is
here-now. Consciousness *is* the limitation—as are
these written words.

December 2, 1963

The discussion this morning began with the
topic of beauty, and the division in India between
religious belief and the sordidness of daily living.
Why it is that the appreciation of beauty and its
wonder has been stultified and channelled—cor-
roded into a series of given patterns. How the
habitual is difficult to uproot, because what is
familiar is not noticed or seen as fresh but accepted as natural and real, and so becomes an *un-
perceived* movement of consciousness—the way of
one's life.

This developed into a search into the vast problem of "what we know," the accumulation already stored in the brain cells; and of why we
want to know, why we each desire our separate
comprehension of everything. This inquiry led to
the realization that every investigation begins with

what we know—that we start with the known and
go on from there. We don't examine the known,
the familiar. The known is this entity's (my) accumulation—the known is "me." We begin with
it as the base, and so are never free.

December 5, 1963

The days slip by with extraordinary rapidity.
Today's discussion (10 A.M. to 12:30) slipped by in
a flash. It related only, though not exclusively, to
why there is not "direct action"; why the mind
deals in ideas, why we ensure *inaction* by translating perceptions into ideas and plans, ensuring
that there is no direct action, only the development of ideas, of techniques, and possibilities, all
of which is delay, and merely "creates" a future
in which action may occur.

Krishnaji's astonishing ability to open up a
question at many levels simultaneously! This
discussion was on why idea is introduced, following perception of anything, and it also included
what it is to cooperate *without* idea. Which means
not only *without* a common purpose (which is
simply a common desire, a common motive), but
to meet, match, and mingle with another at the
same time on the same level, with the same intensity, *without* motive; to be with another, or a
group, in communion.

Also, into this discussion came the question of
schools, and the need to build up a climate of attitude wherein the need of children to be free is
the first consideration. Not the educator, not the
administration, but the children. That *the teacher,
the administration*, etc., is *one* wheel, and the
children the other. In this sense, both are impor-

tant and interdependent, but the teacher and the administration are important only in that they free the children. He suggested this morning that a man go around India, awakening the possibility of educating children for freedom, in freedom.

It could be a new movement in Australia.

December 7, 1963

Today I talked with Madhavachari, and he has arranged for me to go to Rishi Valley for the talks and discussions there; so I leave Rajghat on the 14th, and arrive at Rishi on the 17th of December.

It is astonishing what is happening, the change in the quality of perceptive thinking, the simple clarity into all the passing nuances of thought and behavior, the extensional awareness, without blockage, the "flowing with" in full, free, open simplicity.

Yesterday in the talk to the children (the last talk to them at Rajghat), Krishnamurti began by developing the theme we have been opening up in the small daily discussions, of giving *space* in the mind so that understanding can occur. He began by saying that to see anything clearly, there has to be space between you and that thing, whether it is the other side of the river, or a feeling, or an idea, a flower, or a person—space without the intervention of anything else, space in the physical world (distance)—space in the mind, an area of stillness without thought, feeling or any reaction—space in which perception can grow, in which seeing can take place. Space is timeless and total. In this openness, creativity has its being.

He talked of aggression, of how we brutalize

ourselves and others. At first I thought he was overemphasizing the aggressiveness of human beings until he opened it up, and I saw that all attempts to free oneself, or to *do anything* is an act of aggression; that all control is aggression, be it of anger or annoyance—and at subtler levels, all thought is an intrusion, and so a bruisng and blurring of "what is."

At Dr. Chak's invitation I have talked twice to the children at their early morning assemblies, and find them a great delight.*

At one group discussion with Krishnaji in his house, he talked of waking up in the morning and letting the body "tell what it requires"—sensing what it feels to be indolent, to stretch, to twist, and to move with its movement or its need to remain quiet. Instead of waking up and the mind immediately going into its patterned procedure of rising and doing whatever is the routine habitual procedure—to invite the body to let its needs be known so that at the very beginning of wakeful consciousness each day there is no division between mind and body. It is not that the body dictates to the mind, or the mind dictates to the body, but that the whole being and body are aware together, completely as one. Then movement for the day begins as a totality.

December 9, 1963

Yesterday—Sunday—was the last talk. The exodus has been general. There has been a change in travel dates. I leave now on the 11th and it will

---

*Dr. Chak was the principal of the Rajghat School in 1963.

take two days and nights aboard four trains and a long bus ride to reach Rishi Valley, all being well, on the night of Friday the 13th. This going to Rishi has been arranged through Madhavachari—who I now discover is a remarkable man, and perhaps a closer link with Krishnaji these days than Rajagopal. This morning at 5:45 I called at his house, to find him working. With quiet grace he put aside the manuscript he was checking, and we talked for half an hour (they're up early in these parts). Around 6:15 I walked on down to the river to see the sun rise and to greet the coming day—and there, on the mud bank, right at the junction of the Varuna and Ganges Rivers, I saw a dog tearing at some object. I took a closer look. It was a human body, mostly skeleton, but still with patches of flesh. An astonishing sight, right there at the water's edge! Nearby a man was washing himself and gargling the water. Three crows on the ground waited for the dog to eat his fill, so that they could have theirs. The bare bones of the legs dangled about as the dog tore at the head. The harsh basic reality of a body after death gave me a strange feeling of the transience of life.

The red sun rose on the scene from the horizon across the river, the Ganges. In the ancient Hindu temple fifty yards away the monotonous bell was ringing. A boatload of forty women on some sort of pilgrimage was being rowed up the river (in near the bank to escape the undertow) by one man, and the women were singing (chanting). The rower, straining to make slow headway against the current, pulled himself right off the seat to complete each stroke.

Everything is brutally stark here. Human life is regarded as cheaply as animal life is to Westerners. The culture is totally different from life as we know it, and cannot be comprehended by meeting it with conditioned eyes and responses. Strangely, much of my conditioning seems to have evaporated into thin air, so that I see all this without distress, almost as though it were an everyday occurrence and merely of passing interest. But it does make me wonder about Indian people—in the sense that no one cares. Oh, they will spend time and care on designing and knitting beautifully patterned cloth and on making fine jewelry, and they have an enormous, flowing affection for family and friends. But the very weight of numbers—thirteen million more births than deaths every year, a hundred million more mouths to feed every eight years—wipes out the individual Indian's concern for the plight of other human beings.

Sleep

Ever since the last talk with the children at Rajghat, I have been aware of an inward peace when
I awaken and of the extraordinary nature of this
daily phenomenon itself—coming into consciousness on waking, and drifting away as sleep quietly vaporizes consciousness. So common is this
transition that for most of my life I gave it no attention. When I would lie down, my purpose was
to sleep. I paid little heed to the process itself.
And on waking, my consciousness quickly became
engaged with the tasks for the day, or habit
automatically took over and I began the usual
round. I had been missing the miracle, overlooking the natural twice-daily opportunity to uncover
a mystery of existence, the birth and death of consciousness, of understanding, of being, that mo-
mentary mutation of consciousness *as it is
actually happening.*

For millennia human beings have meditated,
prayed, contemplated, watched, studied, written,
read, and worked to find the answer to the riddle
of existence, the essence of reality, the source of
being. Thousands of techniques have been used—
from Zazen to Hatha Yoga, from climbing Mt.
Everest to fasting, from entering a monastery to
making a million dollars.

The fact is that to be aware of the daily awakening of consciousness each morning and its fading into sleep, into infinity, in the evening, I don't have to develop a system or learn a technique. The transition happens for everyone with every rotation of the earth. I don't have to wait until the "I" dissolves or disappears as the body does at death. The means, the opportunity is already here in the daily transition of waking and sleeping. No practice is needed. It happens naturally; is inherent in daily life.

So I began to give "the transition" an opportunity to expand. I began to watch the beginning and the ending of consciousness each day. And wondered why I had not noticed this ever-present chance before—this transformation into life (consciousness) and transformation out of life (unconsciousness). What I had been searching for always had been sought as though it were not already here. I had not noticed because I had not looked into the actuality of waking and sleeping. I had placed comprehension away in the future.

Watching this wondrous, twilight state of mind with its dreamlike clarity is far vaster than an individual experiencing. It happens throughout the phenomenal world as the sun, and so dawn and dusk, sweep around the globe. Everything is most alive during the two brief daily transitions. At dawn the world is filled with activity and birdsong. Not only are the day creatures awakening, but the night animals are actively settling down. At dusk the process is reversed. At noon and midnight, all activity is less.

Watching the twice-daily transition into and out of life (or consciousness), into and out of death (or unconsciousness), into being and out of being, reveals the process itself: When I lie down, I want "out," oblivion, sleep. When I awaken, I am concerned not so much with what is happening, as I am with projecting what I have to do or want to do, and the ways to achieve these results. Moreover, when consciousness slides away into sleep, so does "the world," along with "me"; we disappear together. And, of course, it is *not* only at dawn and dusk, but endlessly, all the time, that consciousness keeps changing, coming and going.

Letters from Rishi Valley

December 15, 1963

The countryside around Rishi Valley is truly magnificent with its granite hills, cultivated valleys,
and stark beauty. Most wonderful of all, I am in
the guest house, along with three other men and
Krishnaji, whose rooms are upstairs.

I am in luck: with work, this is the opportunity
I have been waiting for, to break through all the
patterns at one stroke; to go beyond that small
area of life, the intellect, into total existence, total
life; to live fully with every movement and every
nuance of life.

December 17, 1963

This morning was the first talk with the children,
immediately after breakfast, at 8:35. Krishnaji
spoke for half an hour and then answered their
questions. He explained what intelligence is: that
it is not being clever, not the astute mind, the cal-
culating mind, the knowledgeable mind, not the
mind that cultivates its own talents, as a man tills
his own field as separate from all the earth. Intelligence is the ability to understand all this.

Krishnamurti was asked by a young girl: "How
do you find out what you want to do?"

He replied that this is a most difficult question because it involves the whole of one's being to discover what is the innermost necessity of a boy or a girl, or for that matter, for a man or woman. He went on to relate this need to discover what one will do "for the rest of one's life" to intelligence, saying that intelligence is love—and to discover what love is, what you love doing above all else, what you are prepared to let go, demands the utmost intelligence. Very few discover what it is they need to do, and that intelligence is love, and love is sensitivity to everything.

December 20, 1963

The days have slipped by. I take long, long, walks—up Rishi Konda (the mountain to the west, after which the valley gets its name), through the surrounding villages, and into the mountains on both sides of the Valley—and attend Krishnaji's discussions with the teachers (on Sundays and Wednesdays) and with the children (on Tuesdays and Fridays). I also spend time writing a little, talking to the children, playing tennis with them, and in the evening, watching the dance dramas of the eldest students under the great banyan tree. These dances are superlative; the girls have been training for six to eight years—throughout their whole schooling—with the South Indian bharatanatyam dancer Miss Meenakshi, who directed the Indian dance troupe that performed at the First Edinburgh Festival of 1961. They are thoroughly professional, in fact, better by far than any dancers I saw in Bombay or Delhi last year. The programs are made miraculous because of the setting, as all performances are danced under the banyan tree. This magnificent tree, ninety feet high, with a girth of around sixty feet, is a perfect backdrop. A famous tabla player and a drummer and a flautist were brought up from Madras and spent weeks in rehearsal with the dancers. Wonderful! In every way. And the folk dancing!

Apart from the talks, my joy has been the walks—alone in these ancient, rock-clad, granite mountains, long hikes, often eight to ten miles. The sunsets are splendid, and these last three nights the new moon has followed the sun down with Venus into Rishi Konda.

December 23, 1963

Life in the valley moves quietly and with a rhythm of its own. Krishnaji and two of the teachers, Venkatachalam, the vice-principal, and the house master of the Golden House—the *small* boys' house—are practicing the Vedic mantras. These are intricate tonal and rhythmic chants from way back, probably more than three thousand years ago. Krishnamurti is rehearsing with that untiring, interested persistence until every phrase, every nuance of meaning and tonal expression is mastered.

Last night I walked with Krishnaji through the dusk into the early evening. I had wanted to talk with him about what to do back in Australia, but there was no heat in me about what is to be done—so we walked—and the changing lights in the sky and the rhythm of the walk took over. We scarcely talked at all.

December 24, 1963

This morning Krishnaji talked to the children from 8:35 to 9:25. It was an object lesson for anyone in "how to teach."

The little ones, six and seven years old, were restless and coughing, so Krishnaji played with them by asking *if* they could sit still, to see how long they could sit without moving their eyes. Immediately most began coughing self-consciously even more than before, and after thirty seconds, settled down, eyes closed. After a minute or so, Krishnamurti began talking again.

Unlike the older children, who were attentive, the young ones soon became restless once more. Krishnamurti sat watching them with amusement. When most had become aware that he was not talking but watching them, they quieted and he again asked if they ever played at being still. Did they know if they could sit still? "Let's do it." After, say, two minutes of comparative peace, he said "Don't you find it very pleasant, just for a little while, to be still, to be quiet?" And he went on to talk about what it is to be natural, to react without the heavy centered weight of habitual restlessness.

In each talk, each discussion, he moves only from fact to fact. When an idea intrudes, rises in someone's mind and is expressed, he goes into it in detail, interested to see what has arisen, so that the whole of this "reaction" is given room to blossom, to be seen, and perhaps be understood. Even the least thought, the least feeling which apparently sidetracks a discussion is investigated, so that all the blocks are permitted to open out into consciousness, to develop and reveal their nuances and meanings.

At lunch in the dining hall, some older students and I were discussing the morning's talk and the thoroughgoing way in which Krishnaji opens up questions—the meticulousness—when one student remarked that he couldn't now recall a flash of understanding he'd had during the talk. He said that the most astonishing thing was that, while Krishnaji was talking, he had had a vivid insight into the source of the "self" and "self-consciousness." But now, "for the life of him," he couldn't recall what it had been.

We found we had all had similar lapses of memory. As we talked it became clear that such "lapses" can be an emptying out of the past, and as there is nothing real left to remember, so there is *nothing remaining to be recalled*—not even the insight that had released the store.

December 25, 1963

A most extraordinary thing happened today. The teachers met with Krishnaji in the upstairs room of the guest house facing south. We had talked for a while when a school teacher asked a question about the "comparative spirit."

Krishnamurti said, "To compare is to destroy both." An American, Gordon Young, thought Krishnamurti merely meant comparing two pupils. Krishnamurti went on, "I mean the one who compares and the two persons or pupils or situations which he is comparing. Comparison indicates no understanding. When one views the whole map of man, his divisions and comparisons, what is one's response?"

For an hour he probed and questioned us (we were thirty-five: twenty-five teachers and ten Westerners); one said "despair" was his feeling.

Another said "futility," when "one realized what must be done." Another answered that to be aware of all this was crushing; that she felt quite impotent.

Over and over Krishnamurti asked what humanity is doing. He pointed out that all our knowledge, our study, our experience is not answering this question, and he inquired, "What is your total response to this total question of man—comparison?" He emphasized that we have to find an immediate and total answer to the whole problem, the whole situation, and not to carry it forward as a problem. A crow called. We were all stabbing at answers, partial answers, incomplete responses, individual reactions. Krishnaji asked, "What is it like to listen? How do you listen to that crow? Do you listen emptily, like an empty vessel, an empty cup, or do you hear it along with all the other sounds? Do you name it? Do you suppress all ideas, feelings—leave them in the bottom of the cup and with the remaining emptiness on top, with that empty remainder at the top of the cup, hear the crow? Can you listen to the sound of the crow, see the flower in total emptiness? Are you totally empty when you view the whole problem of man, and in that total emptiness see the heart, the core of what man is doing—what he is—and so, all that he does?"

We sat in silence; quietly Krishnaji rose and walked away, leaving the whole problem and its resolution with us in a room now empty of his presence and stimulation. The state of emptiness remained. No one moved for some time; the state of unenclosed, uninfluenced emptiness, of stillness, of silence, lived on.

In that hour the whole problem of man's confusion and struggle dissolved into stillness... temporarily.

December 27, 1963

> *Life is a free and rich experience*
> *to be lived, not struggled with.*

The question of this morning's discussion was made by a brilliant final-year boy, Papaji, when he asked: "What makes thoughts and feelings keep coming—keep repeating?"

Krishnamurti: "What you like, you seek to repeat; what you dislike, you seek to avoid; this sets in motion the repetitive habit-pattern of thinking-feeling. All your relationships are based on like and dislike.

"Thoughts and feelings cannot come to an end while you perpetuate the habit—the continuance of your likes and dislikes; only when you understand the whole content of a like or a dislike is there no carryover. So, watch the feeling, the response—every feeling, every response."

Then Krishnaji said, "May I ask you a question? What is beauty?" When no one replied he asked: "You understand the question? Look at that tree. How do you see it?" No reply.

"When you watch the road leading up the valley, is it beautiful? The skyline of the horizon against the sky, is that beautiful? The dirt on the road, the face of the man you pass, which is twisted, do you call that ugly or beautiful?"

The boy Papaji said, "It is beautiful if it gives me a feeling of joy, of happiness."

Krishnamurti: "And it is ugly if it gives you a feeling of distaste? But is it ugly just because you

don't like it? Is beauty dependent on your response—if you do not see is there no beauty?''
Again he asked, ''So what is beauty?''

Papaji was now really into the question. He
glanced at the tree, but it was clear that he was
seeing inside himself. Presently Papaji said,
''Beauty is sensitivity?''

Krishnamurti: ''You are sharp and perceptive.
Sensitivity is beauty. If you sit quietly, or when
you walk, listen to every sound. Let them all
come in; hear their multiple beauty. Do it now.
Sit quietly, close your eyes, or leave them open—
and hear what is going on about you. [We sat for
a minute]. . . . You heard that distant crow? The
slapping of the rock with the wet cloth, the movement of the boy next to you, or the one away from
you; the very far and the very near sounds. This
listening cannot be learned from a book, or from
anyone. It cultivates a quick, vivid sensitivity;
listening sharpens the senses and the mind. Listen
to every sound, let every sight come in, every sensation. Sensitivity is beauty, and to be sensitive
you have to be done with 'likes' and 'dislikes.' I
like this, I dislike that—sound, sight, feeling,
idea, person. All come into consciousness and
reveal themselves as they are. This IS the sense of
beauty. It is total and immediate.''

January 1, 1964

Today was the deepest, most freeing discussion
with the teachers. It went through and beyond
many crucial levels, and fortunately I recorded it.

Krishnamurti began by asking what we wanted
to discuss. One teacher said, ''How do we teach
children so that they are ready to face tomorrow?''
Another asked, ''What is meditation?''

Krishnamurti said, "Let us combine the two questions, for in the answering of the one there will be meditation."

First we explored what it is to live in an isolated beautiful valley like Rishi, apart from the main flow and stimulation of world events. We saw that no matter where one lives, the sources of information—radio, newspapers, TV, periodicals—are the same, but that in this valley away from it all, there is the tendency to think of what is happening elsewhere as only relatively important, to narrow everything down, for interest to be focused only on local things and happenings. This leads to a certain shallowness of outlook and interests, and to a tendency to gossip about people on the campus—a preoccupation with the commonplace. This is because there is less diversion, less distraction, fewer amusements and more concentration on a narrower field; which means that any inherent tendency to character weaknesses in individuals here tends to be emphasized and exaggerated. So more care needs to be taken of the tongue, eyes and ears; otherwise these frailties, these tendencies, and peculiarities in isolation can lead to abnormalities, even to madness.

Krishnamurti then said, "As to teaching the children, preparing them for tomorrow—there is no tomorrow."

This came as a shock.

Krishnamurti went on: "There is chronological time—tomorrow follows today—but there is not development towards tomorrow. Now, when this statement 'There is no tomorrow' is put, what is your response?"

One young American woman said, "It would be dreadful if there were no tomorrow!" Another, when directly questioned, replied, "If there is no

tomorrow, then there can have been no yesterday.'' And a third said, ''Then there must be only
the present.''

Krishnaji: ''Please listen to the question. Don't
give answers. Someone has said, 'There is no
tomorrow,' and you immediately respond with
words, with concepts; you speculate as to what
the answer is. All your answers are reactions. Are
your conditioned pasts meeting the statement? It
doesn't matter who has said, 'There is no tomorrow,' or whether the statement is true or false.
You yet do not know. Give the question space in
your minds, so that it can grow, develop; so that
you can see its full implications, its meaning, its
substance—if it has any.''

To the American woman, Krishnaji said, ''When
you said, 'It would be dreadful if there were no
tomorrow—it meant there are things you want to
do—have a baby; complete your career; understand all that you do not now understand. You
meant you want time—time in which to do all
these things and to experience them, to complete
them. These are all reactions of your past, of your
conditioning, projected into the future—into what
you hope will be the future.

''And you, sir, said, 'Then there must only be
the present'; but the statement 'There is no tomorrow' has nothing to do with the present. What is
your response, not in words, not your conceptual
reaction, but what is your immediate *seeing* in the
statement, 'There is no tomorrow'? What do you
find taking place in you?''

Krishnaji waited while we listened inwardly to
the question. Then he said, ''You discover, don't
you, the past; the reaction, the response, whatever
you like to call it, comes up out of memory, and
is intensified.''

Someone asked, "What do you mean by intensified?"

Krishnaji: "What rises is intensified: a pain or a
sight or sound is intensified, becomes more vivid,
the moment you give attention to it. So what
arises in the mind in response to the statement is
a response from the past. Now let us go slowly,
step by step. What do you say now?"

Another asked, "Can the mind see anything but
the past? Isn't the mind only the reflection of the
past, and nothing more?"

Krishnaji: "What do you mean by the mind?"

Reply: "The whole mind, the whole being, including all feeling, sensitivity, thought, experi-
ences, awareness, memories—everything."

Krishnaji: "Let's go on from there. The total
mind includes all that; the whole of one's being—all that you are conscious of, and all that of
which you are unconscious. Now, when the mind
is confronted with a question, a statement, any
question, any statement, any fact or falsehood,
what is your response? And the statement we are
watching is, 'There is no tomorrow.'

"The past, which is the mind—and there is
only the past—responds. Anything that occurs in
you is the past rising to meet that statement, that
challenge. Any thought, any feeling, any concep-
tion of or about tomorrow is illusion—is not fact.
You do not know tomorrow. You know nothing
about tomorrow. The only fact in you is your own
reflection, from the past. AND THERE IS NO
PRESENT. Watch it carefully, openly, accurately.
What is the present? Any reaction to the present
is the past responding to, operating in, the present. Any response is the past, the old memories,
conditioned accumulation, evoked by the question. Watch it! Listen with your whole attention.

All you observe, all you see is the past and only
the past—and that's all there is—the past. Is the
observer different from his past—and is the past a
series of remembered highlights, memories, or is
it a total thing—though only parts of it are seen?

"Is the past whole, or is it seen fragmentarily?
And is the observer of the past, of the mind—is
that observer who is the past, different from what
he is observing? The observer is the past. There is
only the past, only the accumulations. The accumulation is the mind, and that is all. The observer, the mind, the accumulations, the
responses, the past, is all there is."

Krishnaji paused, and we watched, letting the
meaning, the implications of this unfold.

Then he said, "*This seeing is the present*—and
this seeing has no tomorrow—and the past has
gone. This empty, still state is without past or
future. This dissolution of the past is transformation, is freedom. This perception frees the total
past, and the *ever-new present is.*"

After a long, long pause, he said, "So there is
no tomorrow, and this is meditation."

Everything was still. Though there were bird
calls and activity outside, movement within the
room was suspended, vividly alive.

The resonance remains in me, not as a continu-
ation, but as an evanescent reality.

This is a summary of a two-hour discussion
taken from the tape. Krishnamurti was so inwardly alive that every flicker of feeling showed in his
face and body movements.

January 6, 1964

The question which has been with me ever
since Rajghat relates to hearing Krishnaji's state-

ment, "Why don't you start awakening India, a climate of awakened attitude towards education." It had occurred to me then, at Rajghat, that such action might be taken in Australia. Yesterday I mentioned this to Krishnaji, and he said, "Let's walk one evening and talk about this."

This evening we walked all the way to the main road and back, and although I brought up the matter, Krishnaji seemed uninterested, and I again realized that there was no fire or determination in me, that I was looking for something to do, some work which would be interesting and worthwhile. The whole *idea* was a kind of speculation, without deep significance—an alternative to working for the Australian Broadcasting Corporation—a better way of living and working, a comparative possibility, a choice. So, naturally, Krishnaji's response reflected my lukewarm proposal.

On the return, as we came to the stream, he said, "Have you considered teaching, and in teaching, discussing and learning with others?"

The question came as a surprise. I have never taught. I shall talk with Krishnaji about this in Madras, about the possibility of talking, teaching, and learning with others. I want to explore further what listening is, and speaking out of a state of mind that does not begin with information and past knowledge.

January 11, 1964

This morning there was a discussion with the whole school—teachers and students together. The little ones squatted up front close to Krishnaji and were, as usual, restless. The older students were seated on chairs, attentively quiet. Krishnaji talked for ten mintues about education, what were they being educated for, about the immense social problems in India, and finally asked directly, "What do you want to do with your lives?"

There was the usual reticence to draw attention to themselves by speaking. Then a final-year student talked about the difficulty of getting a job, and the vastness of this problem in overpopulated India. The discussion came alive when one small boy—he turned out to be eleven years old—challenged Krishnaji's question. He asked, "What can one boy do to change the world? The problems are so big, what can one boy do?"

He was seated directly in front of me and fifty feet from Krishnaji, who immediately focused on the boy whose questions had gone to the heart of the problem, "What could one boy do with his life?"

As I recall, the dialogue went like this:

"Let us begin small, with ourselves here at the school in this beautiful valley. Here you are related to your teachers and your schoolmates—and at home with your parents, brothers and sisters, friends. This is your world. Begin with the world you know. What can you do to change this, the actual world of your daily living?"

Immediately, the boy replied, "I could get to know them better."

K.: Yes. Do you ever have fights? Or get angry?

Boy: Sometimes, yes.

K.: That's something you could look into. Uncover what makes you get angry. You could do that, couldn't you?

Boy: Yes, but that won't change the whole world.

K.: How do you know? [We sat silent.] I've

been told some of you are studying the beginning of Western civilization. The history of Greece.

Boy: Yes, we are.

K.: You've read about Socrates.

Boy: The philosopher—yes.

K.: He did not talk to great crowds. He took no active part in public affairs. It is said he talked only to small groups of students, not more than five or so at a time. He didn't even write down the conversations, what was said. It was Plato who later recorded these dialogues. Socrates was no Pericles addressing the assembly in the Parthenon proposing plans to change Athens or the world, or society. He did not talk about implementing social programs. Socrates [was] inquiring into reality, into the human consciousness with a handful of friends; yet [by] investigating inwardly, he was to change Western civilization, far, far more than the lawmakers. Begin small, understand the world in which you live. Let what you see and say and do be the real beginning of change.

Afterwards, I talked with the boy. He had been profoundly affected by the outcome of his challenge. He had seen not only into himself, but had had a dawning realization of what he could do; of what had happened when he challenged and then held to what he saw and understood, when he did not defend his information, but tested it.

Function and a Deceptive Shadow

During the 1960s and 1970s I was to travel the Indian "Krishnamurti circuit" eight times, usually beginning in New Delhi, then on to Rajghat, Madras, Rishi Valley, Bangalore, and Bombay. On the first two sojourns, I took an Akai recording machine. From 1965 to 1975, I brought a Nagra— loaned by the ABC. So the recordings were of top broadcast quality.

I went to listen, to experience, and also to record the public talks and discussions and some of the group discussions held in the residences where Krishnaji was staying. These tapes were sent to Sydney. Excerpts from the tapes were broadcast nationally over the Australian Broadcasting Commission in a weekly program called "Scope." The full tapes were played on a regular weekly basis at the central location in Sydney, the Wayside Theatre. Once videos were produced, these replaced the audio presentations at the theatre on a monthly basis.

Apart from the 1962/63 winter when Krishnamurti did not come because of the Indo-China border war, my Indian sojourns were pilgrimages, refresher courses, and delightful holidays, which formed a kind of biannual structuring of my life, each three-month visit giving it renewed impetus and meaning. And the spinoff from this was the work in Australia, the dissemination of Krishnamurti's books, tapes, and information across the continent.

In a sense, two parallel streams were in operation in me. One was the work, the function itself—the other the status and the feedback which resulted from a recognition among those concerned that something of importance was being done. But a shadow gradually accumulated as acknowledgment of the work widened, and more people became interested.

Power corrupts. Simply to see it and to deny it is not enough. Some assumed that I had a special link with Krishnamurti. Yet there was none, apart from mutual remembrance and esteem, and my heightened awareness in his presence. This is my relationship.

Just as there are "in" jokes which are only understood and appreciated by those involved in a particular occupation, so there is a belief that those who are *not* in the know must work through those who are. In a very real way, recognition not only goes with function, but it is assumed that these "special" persons, through their associations and links, have access to sources of control. The hierarchical pyramid power structure is inherent in human tradition and thought. It is a future-geared activity that nurtures ambition and breeds devotees, sycophants, and coteries of like-minded people, as well as devious behavior—both overt and concealed, fooling others along with ourselves through self-trickery and illusion, and the illusion of leaders and followers.

Krishnamurti denies the master-pupil relationship and affirms that individuals can be free from authority. Even so, the experience of being touched by his astonishing energy can evoke the age-old behavior of looking to another to learn about oneself.

Often the first experience of Krishnamurti is dramatic. One reads or hears some "truth" and it reverberates through one's being. Sometimes it begins simply as a fresh insight into self, pointing to a vaster perspective of life. Thus is born the desire to learn more—read more books or listen to tapes and perhaps meet the man himself. So emerges the devotee and a euphoria that can go on and on.

The "search" has thus become dual: first, what he says, then the listener/hearer's comprehension and behavior.

The duality is in looking *out*, hoping for guidance, and looking *in*, hoping for change which leads to overlooking, looking out *over* the present and missing the immediate living reality.

A Prediction

New Delhi, 1967

One morning at the Shiva Rao home in New Delhi, I was recording a small-group discussion when an extraordinary prediction was made casually. As often happens in the intense explorations, a point is reached when there is no answer, when the known is exhausted, no new leads appear, and the essence is still hidden. A halt had come—yet no solution. Everyone was alert, looking, and waiting.

I was stuck, as, apparently, was everyone else. Krishnaji suddenly smiled, "I've got it!" It came out lightly.

Although Krishnamurti was the focal point of these discussions, everyone was directly involved in the inquiries, working with and through the group. In a very real sense human consciousness was at work; we were all sharing and contributing, each according to our capacity and comprehension.

Krishnaji's delighted "I've got it" prompted Pupul Jayakar's "I haven't."

For a few minutes Krishnaji talked about the way we let him do all the work while we waited

for his answer. Then he said, "When I'm dead
you will have to do the work. So do it! Find out
for yourself, now!"

Pupul replied pragmatically, "But *you are
here*!"

Krishnamurti retorted, "I'm dead!" and he sat
back, hands raised, palms facing out, unmistak-
ably indicating that he was out of it, that the
problem was ours.

We sat silent for a while. The discussion's impetus had dropped. Thrown back on myself, I was
looking inward. But Pupul, pursuing her search
and wanting to hear Krishnaji's insight, was
adamant.

"You're not dead. While you are alive and
talking . . ."

" . . . and I will be until I'm ninety-two." It was
an inconsequential, inadvertent admission, given
no importance, for he went right on to tell what
he had seen, and what all of us wanted to hear.

A spontaneous, throwaway sentence—"and I
will until I'm ninety-two"—an unstressed, casual
prediction. But it had been said and heard and
recorded. A "chance" prediction made in 1967,
nineteen years ahead of time. Krishnamurti died
at 12:10 A.M. on Monday, February 17, 1986, in
Ojai, California, in his ninety-first year.

The Many Faces of Anger

Madras, 1965-66

The consequences of being somewhat high-strung, as I am, are many: instant sensations, fast reactions, quick movements, rather rapid talking and walking. So, when I notice something needing attention, I straightaway want to act and if it is possible, usually do. This urgency to act is actually a reaction. And, I "hasten" to add, these responses are brief and though vivid soon pass from my consciousness (even if not carried out). Often they provoke similar responses in others, with all the ensuing interactions and consequences.

Take anger, and its many manifestations. I was recording the public talks/discussions and some "small" discussions, then sending the tapes back to the ABC in Sydney. There were always endless delays at the post offices while these packages were maneuvered through the system. Usually registration took two or three hours.

Instead of blowing my top, I tried every artifice: smiling to cover my distress, urging the clerks along, waiting "patiently," resignedly, for the interminable process to end. Every stage of the registration of the bulky packages was done by a

different person. Each operation had to be
checked and rechecked. Of course, I fooled no
one, not even myself, with my antics and attempts
to camouflage my real feelings. It didn't work.
Other customers with time on their hands stayed
to watch and enjoy the entertaining charade.

Nothing altered, whatever I did or refrained
from doing. The two to three hours were standard, and having once been to a post office, when
I returned with another neatly sewn linen packet,
the post office team reenacted the slow farce.
Even after I came to know one or two employees
quite well, they made no concessions to my frustration; the post office crew knew the game, and
played it, or so it seemed. Even setting aside half
a day and treating the whole excursion as an interesting experience did not stop my agitation. I
could not help thinking how futile the Indian
postal system was, that it engaged so many different postal clerks to handle one package—nor how
banal I was, reacting the way I did.

I had watched my behavior and seen that anger
can be the outcome of frustration and frustration
the outcome of will, and will the outcome of a desire to get my own way...and wanting it quickly.
I had seen thwarted achievement lead to impatience, and impatience to anger, and anger to neurotic action or farce. Thus began another probing
into anger and its devious expressions. So every
week I went through this debilitating process.
And I got better at letting my feelings arise and go
by. However, I was not free. In one form or
another, anger arose every time, and it had to be
dealt with. Eventually, I became fascinated by my
performance.

There was no real alternative to posting the

tapes back to the ABC. Besides the inconvenience of lugging them from place to place, and the chance of losing them or having them stolen, there was the hassle of boarding planes with ten, twenty, thirty reels of tape and of having my luggage overweight, and the problem of customs and customs duty on a great batch of tapes on arrival at the Sydney airport.

I asked Momma for an appointment with Krishnaji, and it was arranged. When I arrived, Krishnaji was in the office at Vasanta Vihar. We went through to the ground floor room where the interviews were conducted during that visit. We squatted on the floor facing each other, cross-legged. Krishnaji's steady, inquiring look held the question, "Well...?"

I said I wanted to talk about anger, in its many forms, and the many masks I wore to disguise it. I talked about frustration and the multiplicity of associated feelings. He leaned slightly forward and asked, "Do you really want to go into this the *whole* way, sir?"

Once again, I had that awesome sensation of high apprehension—of not knowing what might come out, what I might have to admit.

"Yes, sir."

He had now asked for, and I had invited, the probing. This is why I had come, and an agreement had been established. I must have been expecting the inquiry to begin gently, at the periphery of anger, with impatience, and then work inward. It was not to be. The first question probed an area I had not considered.

"What is your sex relationship with women?" Krishnamurti had touched a vast reservoir of unconscious energy and urges. For months there had been no sex and no interest, other than delight in women's beauty, movement, gentleness, attractiveness, and the indefinable feminine grace and vapor trails that emanate from them and which elicit my attention. Since I had been in India there had been no overt sexual stirring whatsoever in me. And elsewhere, often for long periods, I felt no sexual arousal, no desire, until some woman would come and the magic awaken.

These and many other flashes raced through my mind. Tell Krishnaji all this? What to tell! What to withhold!

I put the question directly to myself. What is my sexual relationship with women? The implications were enormously wide and disturbing. I watched, recalling, looking, sensing. Krishnaji in his stark, impersonal way, focused my attention.

"When was the last time you slept with a woman?" The direct question required a direct answer. I told him. And immediately I wondered whether there *was any frustration* in me with regard to women and sex that turned to anger? Was anger in me unconscious, a masked sexual desire? He must have sensed this to be so, otherwise the question would not have been put. Clearly, I had to uncover the life-energy-movements, admit them into consciousness, see their operation in my mind-body-being. A real probe was about to begin into the primary causes of male and female tension, into the traditional attitudes and roles, and, particularly, the impulses that I experienced. We probed the links between impatience and anger for the next hour. When the dialogue was over, or rather when my "time" was up, Krishnaji said, "Come tomorrow morning...if you wish. Ask Momma to arrange a time."

So began a series of investigations into anger. On Tuesday, Wednesday, Thursday, and Friday, the dynamics of energy, its flow and blockages, opened out. My desire, from its initial impetus and throughout its whole course, was loosened and unraveled. Anger can come when fulfillment is frustrated, and always there is fear joined to it—the fear of failure that underlies every venture.

Throughout those days and nights I watched the kaleidoscope of reactions and actions and feelings that passed through consciousness. What madness is anger! It can bring temporary release through some neurotic act, but what an enormous waste of energy!

First, when anger is about to explode, I am not concerned with watching what is going on in me. I am much more concerned with getting rid of the distress—dealing with the person or situation which I "know" is causing it. And simultaneously, whatever action I take, fight or flight, I am making and remaking escape routes by which the pain I am experiencing finds an expression. I am avoiding experiencing "the wild flow" itself. As I am not concerned with what is happening inwardly, anger remains hidden, unresolved, and feared.

Energy, expressed as anger, is universally accepted as a natural, phenomenal reaction to frustration and pain. Anger is examined and analyzed—as though it had a *separate existence* and so is controllable. Indeed, the motive for examination is to discover its operation in order to control it. And *who* is the controller? Who is the entity who feels the anger? What is anger? These and many other angles surfaced.

On Thursday we were, as usual, sitting on the floor of the sunlit room when an insight came.

Anger appeared in a totally new guise, as "hurry-sickness." The impatient way I approached issues, problems, tasks. The frantic urgency in me to get it finished—whatever the task. Impatience with others, as with myself.

"Leave anger for the moment. What is impatience?" Krishnaji asked. "What is this hyper-sensitivity?"

I watched, feeling again the kind of urgency that impels me to act quickly, to complete the job as soon as possible. . . .For what? To begin the next task? And again, to hurry impetuously through that? And so on and on. I seem to be constantly active, doing whatever thought dictates. And the recurring question comes up—*who, what* is it that hurries? What is impatience that can turn into anger?

I was highly aware of Krishnaji sitting there. Nothing had been said for some time—yet much was happening. Eventually I looked up. His quiet gaze probably matched mine. We sat for a brief spell, maybe three or four minutes, before I rose and left.

Leaving Vasanta Vihar I walked for a while along the grass flats beside the Adyar River, amazed not only at what had happened—and at the perceptive emptiness of Krishnamurti—but at the impossible-to-describe joy that I felt at having been given the opportunity to "go through patterns of me," and experience the silence and heightened awareness that comes in Krishnamurti's presence.

On Saturday, an arrangement had been made with Rukmini Devi to visit Kalakshetra, the unique Indian art school and center she'd set up on the Bay of Bengal, four or five miles south of

Adyar. As usual, I rode a bicycle. The impact of
the daily sessions with Krishnaji and the resonances that had kept resounding through me were
still operating. I had turned off the southbound
trunk road, and was pedaling through a small village when suddenly it burst through me. The
madness of anger, the emotional explosion that
has no actual substance, erupted, but not outward-
ly. In the *inward* flood I saw the whole anatomy
of violence and the source of the illusion made
real by interpretation, by habit, by translation, by
ignorance.

For a second, consciousness was alight, all
clear. Suddenly it was as though I was hearing
the laughter of the ancient gods, all bellowing
together, wildly amused at the goals, hopes, activities, frustrations, angers, hates, and fears of
human beings. Then came the recognition that the
laughter was mine. What a huge cosmic joke humanity has fallen for, accepted, claimed as
natural, taken seriously. By setting up noble pro-
jects and ignoble wars, incubating plans, expand-
ing when we win, collapsing or exploding when
we fail, we live in a mess of our own making.
Sparse attention is given to the ego who dreams
up, then acts out the illusions, who "experi-
ences" the successes or failures, the human mind
that is never free.

The enormity of humanity's oldest jest blew
right through me—I was laughing wildly, uncon-
trollably. The bike began to wobble. I did not
care. Let it go. I fell with the bike and lay there in
the dust hooting with laughter. A dozen curious
children and some men and women, intrigued by
the spectacle, quickly gathered, curious about this
oddity who, having tumbled from his cycle, found

his own condition amusing. They picked up my bike, straightened the handlebars, helped me to my feet, dusted me down, saw I wasn't hurt, and then shared my joy. I loved them all.

It was so ridiculous. The kids frolicked about, acting up. I was aware of all this as though I were not involved, and in a very real way, I wasn't. Their amusement continued as I mounted the cycle and rode off—vastly empty and amazingly light.

The following day, Sunday, I wrote in my diary, "The anger, impatience, anxiety, hurry-sickness is not to be judged as right or wrong, not to be dealt with or avoided, but to be experienced fully—inwardly. There is no necessity to act it out. It may or may not express itself. Enjoy whatever comes as it comes."

From then on the weekly post office dramas were more like light comedies. It no longer mattered to me, so there was no matching reaction in the staff. My stress and their playacting disappeared simultaneously. They were no quicker, and it still took most of the morning, but now I enjoyed it.

Energy

The next interview with Krishnaji pointed up the
versatility of consciousness. Since the last Saturday, my attention had moved from anger and related moods to energy, and particularly the
transformation of energy, the instantaneous
changes in perception that occur. This I wanted to
examine with Krishnaji.

Once we were seated, facing each other on the
rattan mat, I asked about the variable flow of
energy, the wide diversity of its expression and
the extraordinary interplay between the actuality
of a mood and my consciousness of it.

Krishnaji leaned across and lightly touched my
knee. "Slowly, sir." I was aware I was again running on from one idea to another, one feeling to
another. "Go slowly, sir. Don't miss a step. When
you are walking you don't miss one step, so. . ."
Again I was being made aware that in seeking
answers I was leaping over areas that needed
minute, meticulous attention and which, unless
investigated thoroughly, would remain hidden.

Again Krishnaji was reflecting my hurry-
sickness, my impatience to have the investigation
over and to arrive at an understanding.

In pointing out the falseness of quick, periph-
eral probing, he was turning my consciousness

back into itself, inviting me to examine its actual movement as it was happening. It was immediately obvious that in slowing down verbalization, there was also a slowing of consciousness itself, permitting an observation of the hidden mechanism of my thoughts.

Brief Euphoria

A few days later, though an aura of lightness remained, the euphoria had slipped away. I wondered why the miraculous state that sometimes visits was not my normal, everyday reality, and why it departed. Why joyousness once experienced ever disappears.

With this came the realization that to try to regain this wondrousness was vain; that *"I"* could not do it; that mankind, seeking this ever-elusive freedom, has tried everything. Joy visits briefly, and though it may be sensed, it cannot be created. If it could, society would not be as it is; human beings would have been free and happy long ago. Happiness is not within the realm of the known.

Yet whenever, as now, I address this life-long yearning to be joyous, thinking starts trying to devise means whereby it might be achieved. And always, I begin with what I already know—*knowing* that it doesn't work. It's the old abiding binding dilemma.

Through Momma, an appointment was made for the following morning, and I took "my" problem to Krishnaji. The following is what I wrote immediately after the meeting:

My question was, "What is inner joy, inner happiness?"

Krishnaji paused, then asked, "Do you know

what *outward* joy is? In the colors of the sunset,
in the sight of a beautiful woman or a beautiful
man, a flower, a tree? Do you ever give yourself
to this *outward* beauty?. . . so that there is for the
moment a timeless moment—nothing else? No
thought, no re-creation of a memory—pure joy,
pure pleasure?'' He leaned forward and lightly
touched my knee. ''That joyous pleasure in the
outer *is* the inner. And it cannot be evoked,
worked for. It cannot be discovered. No effort is
required, only *interest*. Interest—*not* in yourself,
not in response, but in the life around you, in
others, in the sky, a man, a woman, a child, in
everything, without translating—*is joy.*''

That night, and through the ensuing days and
nights, the interflow between the outer and the inner continued. The very words ''outer'' and ''inner'' point up the dual way of experiencing, and
so, of describing wholeness in a divisive way.
And more, it clarifies Krishnamurti's statement,
''The observer is the observed.'' When the observer is not making anything of what is seen,
heard, sensed, then the wholeness of the beauty
in the world comes into being.

Krishnaji's piercing clarity, ''That joyous
pleasure in the outer *is* the inner,'' and ''To be interested in the *outer*, without translating, *is joy*,''
again transforms the world, transforms the voyeur,
the beholder.

On a later occasion in Rishi Valley, he said,
''You have finished looking at things outside, and
now you look into 'what is' inside. Watch what is
happening inside. Do not think, but watch. You
become very sensitive, very alert to things outside
and inside. You find that the outside is the inside, that the observer is the observed.''

Told to Me

Often I have asked, what makes this man, Krishnamurti, such an extraordinary human being. What contributed to a mind so awake and clear? A sensitivity so subtle? Were the unique qualities there at birth, or did the esoteric education, the lack of personal conditioning, permit the emergence of this transforming presence in the world?

Here are two stories told to me by Madhavachari and Malati Naroji, who had long and intimate relationships with Krishnamurti.

The Madhavachari Story: A Boyhood Incident

I often accompanied Momma on the long train journeys. From Varanasi to Madras, twice, and from Madras to Bombay. We spent whole days together, the two of us, in the compartment. He had been a top railway engineer and had a lifetime free first-class pass. While Krishnamurti flew from place to place with a light bag, Madhavachari carried the luggage on the train. We had an excellent open relationship, and during these days and nights we talked about everything under the sun, and a great deal about Krishnamurti, the teach-

133

ings, and the work. Sometimes Momma would tell of Krishnaji's boyhood days at Adyar.*

One incident concerning "the dreamy boy," the "otherness" of Krishnamurti as a youth, bears recounting.

After the very private tuition had gone on for some time, it was decided that Krishnamurti should have more contact with the world, and especially with children of his own age outside the confines of the Theosophical Society compound. For a time he attended the Olcott School situated just beyond the main gate.†

One morning his teacher told the boy to stay after school, saying he wanted to go over some of his work. At 3:30 when all the other children went off home, the teacher, forgetting his order, left too. When Krishnaji failed to return from school at the usual time, other children who attended the Olcott School were asked if they had seen him. In the general exodus, no one had specifically noticed where he had gone. A search of the compound was begun. All his usual haunts were checked. By dinner time there was real concern. Had he decided to go somewhere, he would certainly have told someone. Consternation began to grow. Search parties ranged more widely. At nine o'clock, someone finally went to the deserted school.

There, in the dark, was young Krishnamurti, seated at his desk, waiting. Five and a half hours had gone by, and he had not moved.

---

*During the first years after his "discovery," the boy Krishnamurti lived in a house overlooking the Adyar River on the grounds of the Theosophical Society Headquarters.
†The school is still in operation.

He was taken home and given a late supper. Stricter supervision for the dreamy boy was ensured—and a return to tutoring inside the compound.

The Malati Naroji Story:
Krishnamurti and the Dalai Lama*

I had met Malati in Sydney in 1939, gone shopping with her in Colombo in 1949, and had visited her farm outside Bombay in 1950. In 1962, we met again in Ootacamund. Sitting on the steps of the Blue Mountains school late one afternoon,† Malati, who had just returned from six months of working for the Tibetan refugees and had been in close daily contact with the Dalai Lama, presented an intriguing theory.

In talking with the Dalai Lama about his early and unique education, she had perceived a real similarity with Krishnamurti's tuition. The Dalai Lama had been told he was "the light of the world," a reincarnation into human form of the essence of life. Unlike princes and all other born-to-be-rulers whose regents make the decisions, the Dalai Lama "from the very beginning" was informed he was "the enlightened one." That was why he had been discovered. He had shown all the signs. He was not educated in the same manner as other children. The practical, normal teaching approach is that a child does not know but will learn as he grows from those who already

---

*The Dalai Lama was associated with Krishnamurti during the 1930s and again after the 1939-1945 war into the 1950s.
†The Blue Mountains school was begun by Gordon Pearce after he left the Rishi Valley School.

know. From the very beginning—even though he did not know what to do, or what should be done—it was understood that the boy Dalai Lama had the capacity to uncover the truth, that, magically, he was the truth.

Bewildering as this may have been at first, it allowed confidence and a certain quality of inward listening to be the essence of his conscious life. The boy Dalai Lama had been told that clarity, perception, and intelligence were not separate from him, that he embodied "the light."

Malati then said that, basically, Krishnamurti's education from the time he was "discovered" had been, in this respect, no different from that of the Dalai Lama. Krishnamurti too had been told he was "the world teacher," and the vehicle for the "light of the world." Those around him were protectors and nurturers of the hidden flame he embodied.

With this education, the "knowledge" that both boys were already that for which humanity had been seeking through the ages, their attention was not primarily focused on learning things for use in some illusory future, but on what was directly related to the living present. The boys were taught not to look outside themselves for guidance or authority, but to be inwardly watchful. With such "non-education" as their normal pattern, such inwardness, it was no wonder that two exceptional "enlightened" human beings emerged.

An Admonition

Rishi Valley, 1966

At Rishi Valley that year I was invited to lunch with Krishnaji in the old guest house. There were five of us. Someone had given him a pot of special mango conserve, and it was recommended that I taste it. Dipping the small spoon into the earthenware pot, I found the glutenous mixture difficult to get out, and even more difficult to loosen from the spoon onto my plate. In trying to shake it free, I tapped the plate a couple of times before the conserve dropped. As I reached out to put the spoon back into the pot, Krishnaji touched my outstretched arm. "No, sir, you tapped your plate with the spoon," and by way of explanation added, "Momma is a strict Brahmin. Once a spoon has touched your plate, it must not be returned to the jar."

This was said as though Madhavachari were not present. Such directness testifies to Krishnamurti's injunction, "the seeing is the doing"—and points up that there is, in a real sense, no personal connotation in such utterances and acts of his, no personal overtones. The fact is stated and left at that. Make of it what you will: that is your affair.

What Is—Is Sacred

Madras, 1967

At Vasanta Vihar, Greenways Road, Madras, the
magic operated more than anywhere else. It may
be that Krishnamurti felt more at home there.
Maybe there are more people who felt in tune
with the man and the message, whose very listening permitted complete simplicity in what was being communicated. Certainly the atmosphere, the
gardens, the huge trees, contributed, as did the
time of day, sunset; and the fact that he walked
only fifty yards from his house to the low dais.
This of course is guessing, but nowhere else in
the world have I experienced the magical quality
so completely, so often.

One talk in 1967 had a profound impact. The
crowd, two thousand and more, were ready as
Krishnaji walked serenely through the trees to the
low rostrum. The crows were still calling and
cawing, boisterously preparing to settle for the
night. As always, Krishnaji slowly viewed the
whole expectant gathering, recognizing here and
there an old friend. Seated beside the rostrum,
ready to record, I watched all this.

He began: "We keep on ploughing and re-ploughing the same ground—never sowing a seed. We churn the ground over and over, and we do not know what to plant. We have no seed to plant...so nothing grows...."

As the talk developed and the depth of communion grew, it seemed as though the whole audience was mesmerized by the beauty of the voice, the rhythm of the words, the profound penetration, the shared wonder that included all.

He told how throughout history, humanity had searched for the essence of being, the source of life, and asked, "Is there anything sacred? Not in temples or churches or mosques. Not in beliefs, in dogmas. Not in ceremonies or rituals. Not in any symbol. The stone by the side of the road is as holy as any image made by the hand or by the mind. Not through sacrifices or offerings, not by placing flowers before idols or on altars. Put a fresh flower before an object, any object, every day, and soon that object will be seen as holy. Repeat a word or a phrase over and over, and it will very soon be heard as holy. Any word will do— "Coca Cola." Do it, sir, and find out! We plough over and over this overploughed ground, and have come up with nothing—and further ploughing will continue to produce nothing."

"So, is all the searching, the struggling, an illusion? Is it all for nothing? If there is anything sacred—what is it? Where is it?"

Krishnamurti, with two thousand people in tow, listening, sensing, waiting. And then it came. It was there for all to hear, to see, to experience; the most profound, the most commonplace, the most obvious, the simplest perception. "What is—is sacred."

The talk was over. No one moved. Magic spread in the silence. Krishnamurti remained seated, still, as were we all, sharing the wholeness.

"What is"; ever-transforming, ever-present. What is—*is* sacred. Of all Krishnamurti's profound statements, these words were to penetrate me the most deeply. There are vast implications in the uncovering of "what is." Often, as I walk— usually in the morning—the immensity of the present brings me to a halt, and I stand filled with the wonder of "what is": "what is" being the beautiful immediate world, a sense of wonder and wholeness, sheer joy at the extraordinary sharpness and clarity of everything.

What initiates these interludes—temporary endings to the normal stream of consciousness—I do not know. They are usually preceded by a sudden recognition of some pettiness that was engaging my attention. And I hear the words, "what is—is sacred."

What is—is real. I stop...looking, listening, sensing "what is." A new consciousness and a new world emerge.

Transference?

Madras, 1967

There is Krishnamurti—a voice from the silence, a
sage with enormous authority—and Krishnaji, the
listening and responding person.

I had been introduced to an American woman
who was in great distress. She had fallen under
the spell of an Indian guru, had left her husband,
and gone off with the sorcerer to his ashram. After
three weeks, she had returned, disillusioned and
humiliated, to be rejected by her husband. He had
even refused to speak to her. Through a mutual
woman friend, he ordered that she pack her bags
and be aboard the night flight out of Madras that
very evening. The same friend took me to see the
defeated, miserable woman, and I was asked if an
appointment with Krishnaji was possible.

I rode over to Vasanta Vihar, saw Madhavachari, and within the hour both women arrived by
taxi and were ushered in to Krishnaji. I was still
sitting on the porch outside the office when,
about ten minutes later, they came out, both
serene and smiling, and entered the waiting taxi.

As they drove off, Krishnaji walked slowly out
of the doorway. There were tears in his eyes and a
great sadness. "Poor woman," he said, "poor

141

woman." It was as though all the woman's travail had been transferred to him, leaving her tranquil, her pain gone—at least temporarily.

He stood there watching, then took a long quiet breath and his demeanor, his whole physical appearance, changed completely. A kind of release had occurred; the stress had passed. He turned to Madhavachari and, as though nothing had happened, the two entered the house.

Two days later, at the morning public discussion, in the huge ground floor auditorium at Vasanta Vihar, a remarkable incident took place.

I arrived early to set up the recording equipment against the wall in the middle of the hall, beside Krishnamurti's low rostrum. I noticed a man already seated at a vantage place at the front of the stage, a very still, self-contained man, whom I had not seen before. His arrogant air announced he had come, not to listen, but to challenge. Occasionally, at public discussions, gurus and other public figures turn up to test themselves and their ideas against the "internationally revered" Krishnamurti. I guessed that was why he was here.

As Krishnaji came in and seated himself, the man shifted his position just a little. My attention was again drawn to him. His piercing gaze was acute.

Krishnaji, as usual, was quietly viewing the silent audience. And, before he began speaking, he turned away from the microphone and softly said to me, "Sir, would you mind moving just a little forward so that you are between me and that man."

I moved, and when I looked again, the piercing intensity had gone from his gaze. I do not know what happened. I suspect, speculate, that once he realized that Krishnaji was awake to what he was up to—the way a child, discovered in some sly act, is suddenly dismayed and powerless—the guru gentleman had given up; he had become part of the crowd.

Male-Female Wholeness

Bombay, 1968, Dongarsey Road, Malabar Hill

An appointment had been made for a *London Times* Sunday Supplement correspondent to interview Krishnamurti. I was with him in the drawing room when the man and his wife arrived. As on some other occasions, Krishnaji gestured for me to remain, saying "Stay, sir."

Once the formal introductions had been made, I was included as a friendly onlooker. After an hour or so of questions and answers and a lot of note taking, there came an incident that was to transform the occasion. A camera was produced and the *Times* man, having received Krishnamurti's permission, began taking photographs. After perhaps half a dozen shots his wife, noticing the bright light of the late afternoon sun streaming in through the open doorway, looked outside and suggested that a photograph in sunlight might be the one they were after. Gracious, as always, Krishnaji complied, and I followed the three out onto the wide verandah. There he stood, quietly waiting while the camerman decided what composition was wanted.

It so happened that close by the door was a most beautiful life-size statue of the Buddha, so simple in its economy of line, so serene in its portrayal of passivity as to be feminine in its tenderness. Even before I saw the magnificent possibility, it was clear that the photographer had seen and decided the two resplendent heads presented an opportunity not to be missed.

He gestured, "Just a little to your left, sir." Krishnamurti moved and stood, watching, waiting. Never before had I seen his features so composed, with such compassionate delicacy, such essential femininity, such sweet passivity. The two figures made a superbly complete picture. Krishnamurti's tranquility and the stillness of the Buddha statue at his shoulder—both luminous in the afternoon light.

So unexpected, so immense was the impact they made that tears welled up inside me. Suddenly all my self-possession had gone. I stood there with tears trickling down my cheeks. The camera clicked quickly three or four times. The professional had the shots he was after. The session was over. I thought that in the flurry of activity my release had not been noticed. I was wrong, for as Krishnaji turned to walk back into the drawing room I caught his discerning glance.

During those brief moments I had witnessed in Krishnamurti male-female wholeness—masculine austerity and strength and feminine patience and adaptability—revealed in one human being: the immediate and the abiding in one body.

I never saw the published article or what must have been a unique photograph.

Tracing Sounds Inwardly

Rajghat, 1969

During a talk to the students and teachers (and a sprinkling of adults from nearby Varanasi), Krishnaji's voice was blurred out by the roar of the goods train rattling its slow way across the iron railway bridge over the Ganges. He stopped, and we all listened.

When the noise had faded sufficiently, he asked, "Did you resist the sound of the train? Did you try to block it? Did you listen to the sound as it moved through you, trace the sound inwardly in your body? Did it end in you? *Has* it ended in you? Otherwise it is not finished but caught in memory." He went on to talk about listening, the state of mind that is listening. Why do we choose to listen to this and not to that, why make decisions about what we want and do not want to hear, why react the way we do? It was "the teacher" in action: using a real situation to point out what was actually happening in consciousness, drawing our attention to the way we were responding; a lesson in self-awareness, an immediate insight into human behavior.

The Poet

Always when I listen to Krishnamurti or as I read him, beyond the actual phrases yet enhancing their meaning, I hear the melodic beauty of the words, the rhythm, the poetry, the song. There is, for me, a stimulation not dissimilar in its mesmeric effect to listening to superb music; a joyous surrender so pleasant as to bring me a dreamlike euphoria and miraculously, simultaneously, a vividly awakened state.

An Invitation

That winter, 1969-70, Krishnamurti was staying at
Rosie Jayalakshmi's house, and so was I. It had
been fifteen years since he had been in Australia,
and one lunch time the occasion seemed right to
invite him to Sydney again. He replied that he did
not know, as yet, what his itinerary for 1970 was
to be, and gave me heart when he asked, "What
time of the year would be best in Sydney?" I had,
of course, considered this, and how it might be
included in his regular yearly commitments in India, Europe, England, and the United States. I replied, "November," and suggested that rather
than flying from Ojai to India via Britain, that he
fly the Pacific and, after Sydney, jet on to India.

The Sydney sojourn became a distinct possibility when he said, "Write to your friends in
Sydney and get them to write to Mary (Zimbalist)
in Ojai telling her of this conversation, so that she
receives an official invitation. In the meantime,
you write to Mary too, letting her know of the
proposal."

I wrote both letters and posted them that day.
And so it came about.

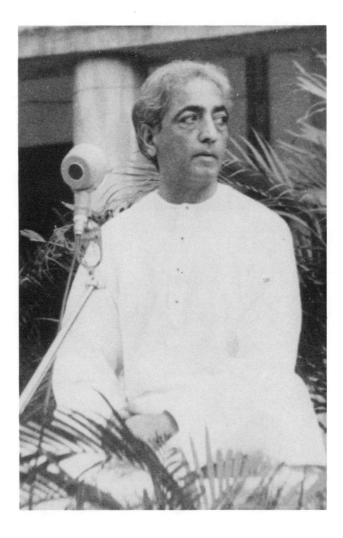

Sydney,
1970

Replaying an Old Fantasy

In November Krishnaji arrived with Mary Zimbalist, and they stayed in an apartment at Manly overlooking the harbor and the Pacific Ocean.

Besides five public talks in the town hall and two public discussions, there were a number of television interviews recorded at the apartment. One interview was to highlight not Krishnamurti's "freedom from the known," but a repetition from the forgettable past. It happened this way:

Like all good television reporters, the interviewer (a colleague working for the ABC) and her producer had done their homework. They had delved into the archival files and found that, fifty years before, a member of the Order of the Star of the East had built an amphitheatre at Balmoral Beach (used for plays and dance performances) on a site with a magnificent view to the east, out through the Sydney Headlands to the Pacific Ocean, and that seats had been sold to hundreds of believers. The fantasy at the time was that, as a kind of second coming, Krishnamurti would walk on the water through the Heads, into Sydney, and that they would witness it. Fantastic! But the story had been reported and the records are in the archives of Sydney newspapers to testify to its validity. Armed with this background, the reporters, including my colleague, had come.

The interview went well. Everyone was pleased. The crew packed up and left. That evening when the program was aired, everyone interested in Krishnamurti who was watching received a real shock.

The producer had come up with a presentation gimmick. The opening shot had my friend standing up to her waist in water at Balmoral Beach, microphone in hand, with the Sydney Headlands as her background, saying, "Today the Indian philosopher, Jiddu Krishnamurti, flew into Sydney by jet; fifty years ago he was to have walked into Sydney through these Heads and on this very water." An attention-grabbing opening, and completely out of character with the interview that followed, which showed clearly that the girl had been deeply moved by what Krishnamurti was saying. However, the opening had indicated a madness in some of his "followers."

When I next saw her, my friend apologized. "It wasn't my idea, but the producer saw the dramatic beginning of me up to my waist in water. Immediately after the interview with Krishnamurti, we drove to Balmoral Beach and, for the cost of a new dress, I waded into the water and did that introduction." So fantasies, once recorded, are perpetuated.

The following day, Mary told me that Krishnaji had seen the interview that night and had made no comment.

The talks were given in the largest public venue in central Sydney, the Town Hall. The overflow crowds at each meeting stood in the hallways, with all the doors open so they could hear.

During one talk a man, obviously a little drunk, made his way through those standing at an entrance and, advancing up the aisle, stood for a while, listening. Then he challenged Krishnamurti, calling out, "No! No! I don't see it that way." It seemed as though he could be a real disturbance—certainly he was a distraction. Many people turned to see what was happening. What to do with a drunken intruder?

Unpredictable as ever, Krishnamurti beckoned the man forward. Rather belligerently he walked up the aisle to the high stage. Some of the audience were becoming apprehensive, even restless. They had come to hear Krishnamurti, not an intrusion by a drunk who shouldn't even be there. For a little time Krishnamurti, in complete control, quietly sat waiting. The tension began to release. The surprise came when Krishnaji invited the man up onto the stage and placed a chair for him nearby. The man sat and serenely listened to the remainder of the talk. Within minutes after being included, he became unnoticed.

The Teacher-Pupil Relationship

At the Thursday morning interview I raised the question of the teacher-pupil relationship. I had been watching my gestures and attitudes, thoughts and feelings, and it was quite obvious that I was not only the pupil learning, but the subject-object of my observations, and so my own primary teacher. One consequence of this realization had been that my reading of Krishnamurti's books had greatly diminished. When I mentioned this to Krishnaji, the following dialogue, which I taped, took place.

As he often does, Krishnamurti transposed our positions. He began, "I am the teacher and the disciple. I discover it is me K. is talking about. The book I am reading is me; the teacher is me." He went on. "You are the pupil, *not* of the book, but of yourself." I said I had seen that to some extent. However, it seemed to me that learning about myself was a way of changing what I am and so a form of *becoming*, of gradual psychological growth, which Krishnamurti denies.

He pointed out that normal living *is* a way of becoming. He questioned the whole process of slowly learning, slowly understanding oneself. "Why does my mind accept the idea of slowly learning, slowly understanding myself? It may not

be slow at all." He went on to say that human beings are conditioned to slow progress and asked,
"Why don't I grasp what is said, what I see, what
I hear immediately? Either you understand it all
or you understand nothing." Here he smiled
delightedly.

I said I didn't feel capable of seeing the whole
all at once, that there was so much to be aware of.

Krishnaji then questioned why it is that the
mind is not open to view the whole movement of
life. Is it because we preselect only what we desire, refusing to take in the whole? Is it because
the brain is so engaged, so focused on our aims
and purposes, that it notices nothing else? He
likened the normal thinking process to looking at
a map of Australia with a purpose, wanting to
find some particular place like Canberra and the
way to it, and not bothering about the rest of the
map.

"All else is distraction to the blinkered mind."
He asked what happens when you enter a room.
Do you look at it in a piecemeal fashion, item by
item, or without intent see the whole room at a
glance, instantly? The whole room is there to be
seen.

For a few moments I pondered the importance
of this way of looking. Krishnaji was right, yet I
still had a query. I said that it did seem to be historically true that the human brain and body have
evolved slowly through time, which implies an
evolution of the learning process.

Krishnaji reached out and lightly touched my
knee. "We're talking of psychological, inward revolution. Direct seeing."

Yes. However, I was determined not to give up
until it was all quite clear. I asked if it isn't right

that we humans get to understand something by thinking it through logically, and if this process isn't an evolutionary psychological development.

Krishnaji smiled and took the wind right out of my sails by inquiring why I stopped there, since it must be clear that intellectual comprehension was not enough. "I understand intellectually that quarreling with my wife or neighbor is destructive, yet I quarrel. Why?"

He went on to question why it is that the brain doesn't see the falseness of accepting logic as the ultimate criterion, why the brain accepts certain logic and then fails to carry it through.

The dialogue ended with Krishnaji pointing out that self-interest is the operative factor, that everything is seen and heard in relation to our own self-interest.

On November 26, Krishnaji recorded a major interview for the ABC National Network. The half-hour program was an inquiry into "Belief." When the floor manager gave "the final windup—thirty seconds to go" signal, the interview went thus:

Q: So you are not setting yourself up as a teacher?

K.: No, no, sir, on the contrary, I say: Be your own teacher. Be your own light. Don't look to somebody else.

Q: And where do you find truth?

K.: Only when a mind, and not only a mind, a life, is completely harmonious, not contradictory. It's only such a mind that can find truth, can observe truth. Truth isn't something abstract. It's here.

Organization

Why Have an Organization to Perpetuate a Teaching?

Human beings are gregarious creatures, and although "self" is everyone's primary preoccupation, most of us also seek warmth and companionship and, hopefully, want to improve communal conditions. Organized groups seek to, and often do, achieve practical social goals, and they nourish personal relationships.

However, Krishnamurti is adamantly against spiritual organizations.

On August 3, 1929, in a talk to three thousand members of the Order of the Star, at the Ommen camp in The Netherlands, he announced his determination to dissolve the Order. A reprint of some passages of this message is pertinent here:

"I maintain that Truth is a pathless land, and you cannot approach it by any path whatsoever, by any religion, by any sect. That is my point of view, and I adhere to that absolutely and unconditionally. Truth, being limitless, unconditioned, unapproachable by any path whatsoever, cannot be organized; nor should any organization be formed to lead or to coerce people along any particular path. If you first understand that, then you will see how impossible it is to organize a belief. A belief is purely an individual matter, and you cannot and must not organize it. If you do, it becomes dead, crystallized; it becomes a creed, a sect, a religion, to be imposed on others. Truth is narrowed down and made a plaything for those who are weak, for those who are only momentarily discontented. Truth cannot be brought down, rather, the individual must make an effort to ascend to it. . . .

"I maintain that no organization can lead man to spirituality. If an organization be created for this purpose, it becomes a crutch, a weakness, a bondage, and must cripple the individual and prevent him from growing, from establishing his uniqueness, which lies in the discovery for himself of that absolute, unconditioned Truth. . . .

"I have only one purpose: to make man free, to urge him towards freedom; to help him to break away from all limitations, for that alone will give him eternal happiness, will give him the unconditioned realization of the self.

"Because I am free, unconditioned, whole—not the part, nor the relative, but the whole Truth that is eternal—I desire those who seek to understand me, to be free, not to follow me, not to make out of me a cage which will become a religion, a sect. Rather should they be free from all fears—from the fear of religion, from the fear of salvation, from the fear of spirituality, from the fear of love, from the fear of death, from the fear of life itself. As an artist paints a picture because he takes delight in that painting, because it is his self-expression, his glory, his well-being, so I do this and not because I want anything from anyone.

"You are accustomed to authority, or to the atmosphere of authority which you think will lead you to spirituality. You think and hope that another can, by extraordinary powers—a miracle—

transport you to this realm of eternal freedom
which is Happiness. Your whole outlook on life
[is] based on that authority.

"You have listened to me for three years now,
without any change taking place except in the
few. Now analyze what I am saying, be critical, so
that you may understand thoroughly, fundamen-
tally. When you look for an authority to lead you
to spirituality, you are bound automatically to
build an organization around that authority. By
the very creation of that organization, which, you
think, will help this authority to lead you to spirituality, you are held in a cage.

"Instead of old spiritual distinction, instead of
old worships, you have new worships. You are all
depending for your spirituality on someone else,
for your happiness on someone else, for your enlightenment on someone else; and although you
have been preparing for me for eighteen years,
when I say all these things are unnecessary, when
I say that you must put them all away and look
within yourselves for the enlightenment, for the
glory, for the purification, and for the incorruptibility of the self; not one of you is willing to do
it. There may be a few, but very, very few.

"So why have an organization?...

"As I said before, my purpose is to make men
unconditionally free, for I maintain that the only
spirituality is the incorruptibility of the self which
is eternal; is the harmony between reason and
love. This is the absolute, unconditioned Truth
which is Life itself. . . . Truth is in everyone; it is
not far, it is not near; it is eternally there."

This absolute statement can so shock the brain
that, for the moment, the self-perpetuating process
stops. Krishnamurti's challenge that truth cannot

be organized, interpreted, or transmitted from one person to another stills the mind, demands attention. As the timeless challenge is allowed to act directly IN consciousness and not be acted upon BY consciousness, a new dimension of living begins. As yeast fermenting changes the form of food, so does truth transform the structure of consciousness.

Forming an Organization

Human associations—organizations—have always
been a source of difficulties. However, there has
to be some sort of skilled organization to arrange
the Krishnamurti talks, disseminate the books and
tapes, develop schools, produce bulletins. For fifty
years across the world, dedicated individuals
under Krishnamurti's guidance had carried out the
work. As in other countries, a small number in
Australia had long been engaged in spreading the
teachings. In Sydney and other cities, as well as
in country towns and private homes, groups met
to listen to tapes. For ten years or so, every
capital city regularly had video showings.

The work was carried out by a few dedicated
people. In particular, Reg and Mavis Bennett insti-
gated some innovative ways of making Krishnamurti known and available to more people.
Huge numbers of paperback editions of his talks
were bought and bound in hard covers and sent to
local public libraries throughout Australia. Every
town with a population of twenty thousand or
more had Krishnamurti books, as did every university, and, for good measure, every jail. Materi-
als were distributed to university libraries in Indo-
nesia, in Japan, and in every South American
country.

After 1968 and the new impetus that came with the establishment of the English, Indian, and American Foundations and the opening of the school at Brockwood Park in England, a renewed interest in Krishnamurti's teachings was apparent throughout the world. One result was the setting up of other legally recognized bodies in several countries.

No such formalization was needed in Australia. There was, however, a block of land at Terranora that had been donated, back in 1927, to the long-defunct Order of the Star, which had been formed around Krishnamurti in his youth. Without a legal entity to receive the title deeds, the property could not be used or sold. For fifty years successive Australian Krishnamurti representatives had failed to get the land transferred to them. It was, in fact, a costly liability because the annual land rates had to be paid.

We were aware that any legal organization designed to receive donations and administer the work would persist even when the need for it had vanished. Organizations are valid only while they perform the specific function for which they were set up. When the task is completed, the structure requires dismantling, perhaps to be reformed by another group of individuals when another need arises. Thus ran our musings. So we wanted nothing fixed, nothing permanent. Could the work continue to be done without *any* formal structure? Well, no; to function on a statewide or national scale there had to be some coordinating body. But how much was necessary, and what was the practical minimum?

There was another important issue. If no legal body was approved and in operation while Krish-

namurti was alive, what happened after his death
would be chancy and possibly confused. Though
rooted in speculation and "fear of what might
be," this matter had arisen and had to be
answered.

We began to consider what had been done over-
seas with Krishnamurti's approval and backing.
There was the precedent of the Krishnamurti
Foundations, established in India, England, Puerto
Rico, and the United States. Whatever we did in
Australia had to be so constituted that it would
work harmoniously with those Foundations. In
1975, I was asked by Mavis Bennett to see what
could be done.* Once again the task of investigating the possibility and feasibility of an Australia-
wide organization was under way.

Legal negotiations were begun, but the freedom
we wanted and the restrictions the law required
were incompatible. Over the years three firms of
solicitors took up the task, an expensive exercise.
None produced a formula acceptable to both the
government and us.

---

*Mavis Bennett was Krishnamurti's representative in
Australia. She followed John MacKay, Spencer English,
and Reg Bennett.

Finance and Funding

The likelihood of establishing an Australian organization, provisionally called "Krishnamurti Australia," gradually faded. We carried on as we had always done. Money needed to finance the operation was supplied in the main by those doing the work.

Over the years at Brockwood and Ojai, I had observed some of the difficulties and ambiguities that fundraising presents. For instance, when there has to be cash in hand *before* the proposed project can begin, raising money becomes the primary objective. Money, which is the means, can appear to be an end. Fundraising, no matter how civil and polite the appeal, smacks of begging. And, like the beggar, the fundraiser has to gratefully accept whatever is offered. Also, begging is false. It fails. It may have worked once, but no longer. There are too many appeals. No one really listens anymore. Another approach is required.

What now needs to be communicated, and clearly, is the new spirit that is awakening in the world. Be in it—participate. Permit those who hear the talks, read the books, and see the necessity to act to know that they can share in the new movement, that it is not only in themselves but also in the world. This sounds evangelistic, enthusiastic, urgent; it is all three. It is also serious, steady, profound, and provocative. For it is a privilege to participate and a joy to share in the awakening and in the work. If you have a skill that is needed, offer it; if you have money available, give it.

Human beings like to grow, to unfold, to work, and to contribute to a successful venture. People don't like to give to an anonymous, amorphous fund that might be used in ways that hold no interest for the donor, so why not let those who want to participate be free to nominate the project to which their contribution is to go? In this way they can see the use of their money, much as those who actually do the work can see the results of their labor. Why not have a fund for those interested in books and in their distribution to libraries, reading rooms, etc.? A fund for audio- and videotapes and viewings? A fund for adult education, for learning and facilities? A fund for a school? A fund for an archive; for a master index?

Such, briefly, was the Australian structure and attitude in 1980.

Colombo, 1980

A Sacrilege

Colombo, 1980

At the invitation of Dr. Adikaram, I went to Colombo for the November talks. As a guest of the
Sri Lankan government, Krishnamurti was given
the red carpet treatment: an official greeting at the
airport and the state guest house, Ackland House
in Union Place, as his residence while in the
country. To his dismay, perhaps, spick-and-span
armed naval guards were on duty at the gates, and
uniformed officers were in the house, for guests of
the state are given full protection in Sri Lanka.

It had been arranged that all Krishnamurti's
public talks would be broadcast over Radio Lanka.
There were a number of prime-time television interviews with ministers of state, and the newspapers made him the subject of feature articles.

On the morning following his arrival, I attended
a large media conference at Ackland House. The
forty or so reporters were quite remarkably defer-
ential, some reverential, in their questioning. One
asked whether Krishnamurti was, in fact, the
twentieth-century incarnation of the Buddha.
Krishnamurti demurred but did not deny. The following day and throughout his visit, most newspapers carried extensive stories about him.

175

During the late afternoon talks and the question-and-answer meetings at the de Silva Theatre, a similar worshipful obeisance was in evidence. In such a devotional atmosphere, it was not difficult to become involved in a misunderstanding.

My earlier links with Radio Lanka, with acoustics and public address systems, had pre-selected me for the task of checking the amplification speakers around the huge, open-sided theatre before each talk. As they began in daylight and continued on after dark, the hall lights and the spotlights on Krishnamurti had to be checked. Night comes suddenly near the equator, making it difficult, if not impossible, to estimate in bright sunshine the electronic lighting needed after dark.

After the first talk, Krishnaji said that the stage spotlights had troubled him, that he couldn't see the audience. As it was essential for him to, Dr. Adikaram asked me to look into this. So on the evening of the next talk, after positioning the microphones and testing to ensure that everyone everywhere could hear, I had to check those spotlights to make certain they would not bother Krishnaji again. The obvious way was to position myself on the purple draped dais exactly where he would sit, and to have the electrician adjust the lights so that, while the audience could see me, I could also see the audience without any discomfort.

It was still full daylight when the electrician, predictably late, turned up ten minutes before the 5:30 start. The theatre was already packed. After a brief preliminary explanation of what I was doing, I seated myself cross-legged in the exact position Krishnaji would take, and from there directed the focusing of the spotlights. When I was satisfied, I

left the stage and went to my seat, conscious that
I had somehow caused offense.

After the meeting, my misdemeanor, my lack of
sensitivity, and the existence of a culture gap concerning my behavior were plain to all. There was
a distinct coolness from those who had previously
been open and friendly. I was now acutely aware
that I had violated a sacred trust: that in sitting in
the Master's place, I had usurped and desecrated
holy ground. I had committed a sacrilege. Sensi-
bilities had been affronted; a number of persons
wanted nothing to do with a man so insensitive.

And, of course, it was true. I had not considered the likely response. I had simply gone ahead
with what I understood had to be done, in the
most practical way I knew. At the time I was
marginally conscious that my action was a mild
status display. In overlooking the inward nudging,
I had permitted "self" to reassert its secretive existence, almost without my noticing it.

Later that evening, when I talked with Dr.
Adikaram and apologized for upsetting so many
people, he too was sad and somewhat bemused by
the distress such an unintended affront had
caused. Later still, I was to realize that far from
being merely an unfortunate error, the incident
was to have far-reaching consequences. One was
that in solving the lighting problem, I had created
another and far more difficult problem of relationship. Many could not forgive me. A few, especially some of those closest to Krishnamurti, did not
speak to me again.

This incident prompted me to ask: To what extent was I, too, a follower, an image-maker, a wor-
shipper, a devotee? And in what ways does devo-
tion to a revered person lead to fanaticism? Was

my own security, my self-image, in any degree
dependent on an unquestioning subservience to
this great man's influence? I began watching myself more closely for subtle traces of reliance on
my idea of Krishnamurti and the teachings to sus-
tain my own self-image, and for any signs of
fanaticism. I realized that my defense of him was
a justification of myself, my judgment, and my
choice of mentor and guide.

The reverberations rang through me for a long
time. Krishnamurti was surrounded by devotees. I
kept wondering why he was not surrounded by
free minds, free people, free relationships. Was it
only the worshippers and the dependents who remained close to him, and those who "heard" and
began the inward work themselves, who walked
away? Was it perchance the very first step in a
realization that there is no model; that freedom is
a state of being, not something to be achieved;
that wholeness and happiness emerge as self un-
ravels, as the sense of separation dissolves? Truth
is indeed a pathless land.

These observations and questions were to come
into acute focus and be fully tested in me some
three years later. Valid as insights are, *nothing
matches a crisis* to halt the flow of dreams, to end
the continuity of self and the past, and to make
things clear in the present.

A few days before Krishnamurti left Colombo, I
went to see him at Ackland House. For two hours
we discussed the ramifications of setting up a
legal organization in Australia, and explored the
possibilities and difficulties of attempting to
operate a school for children in Sydney. Besides
pointing out the rare dedication needed for such
an important venture, and the long-term responsi-

bilities for all concerned—teachers, parents, and students—he made it quite clear that if we did decide to go ahead, the school would have to function wholly in its own right, without using the name "Krishnamurti." Unlike the already established Krishnamurti schools which he visited each year to talk with teachers and students, the Australian school would have to stand on its own. His final words were "work closely with those already involved."

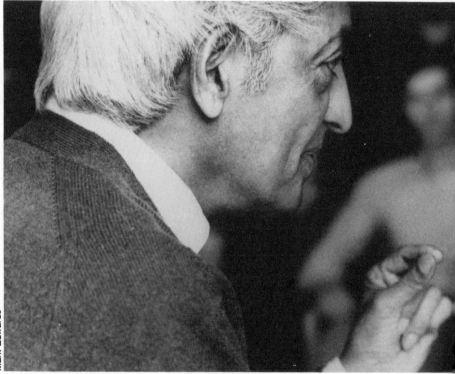

An Ending

Crisis

Negotiations to establish an Australian Krishnamurti organization continued, but with decreas-
ing eagerness. There were still a number of
troublesome standard clauses in the charter, and
one in particular, which read: "The organization
has to transmit any lawful business in and of the
Commonwealth of Australia in the prosecution of
any war in which the Commonwealth of Australia
is engaged."

The offensive statement was mandatory. So be
it. It really would not affect the work. Finally, in
December 1982, a draft of the Memorandum and
Articles of Association was approved. It was not
ideal, but it seemed workable. Copies were made
and sent to Krishnamurti and all the Foundations.

A time bomb arrived in the form of a letter from
Krishnamurti posted from Madras, dated January
13, 1983. In it Krishnamurti wrote that as president of the various Krishnamurti Foundations he
was disassociating himself from "Krishnamurti
Australia." His actual words were, "I expect you
not to use my name with any organization proposed by you." He went on to say that he and
those working with him thoroughly disapproved
of certain clauses in the Memorandum of Association of "Krishnamurti Australia." He asked why

Mrs. Bennett was not the president, saying that such matters should be gone into with great care before I took any further step. He also said that "Krishnamurti Australia" could not by any means take over the properties in Australia belonging to the Order of the Star in the East.

Copies of this letter were sent to all the trustees. We all received a copy on the same day. The effect was stunning. Phones ran hot. That I had been rejected by Krishnamurti was clear. It was also clear that he wanted every trustee to know of his decision. Seven of the eight signatories to the Memorandum and Articles of Association of "Krishnamurti Australia," who were as bewildered as I by what read as an unwarranted indictment, wrote to Krishnaji. The fact was that all of us were implicated.

Days and nights of self-doubt followed, with continuous watching, questioning, and examining, not into what *had* happened, but into self and what *was* happening. Weeks went by before I replied.

In my letter of February 21, I acknowledged his decision to dissociate himself from "Krishnamurti Australia," and his name from any organization proposed by me, and said I would abide by this decision. I wrote of the shock that had exploded through me and of the bewilderment, sadness, and self-examination that followed. I pointed out that the work of disseminating the books, tapes, and information had no relationship whatsoever with the establishment of a legal entity in Australia. In fact, we had not wanted such an organization, nor did we consider one necessary, except for money management. We worked alone, each in our own way, and cooperatively whenever help was needed.

I finished, "It was, indeed, a pity that this happened, that clarity was clouded, that you had to deal with it."

With the posting of the letter, I felt resigned to the reality that I was out of the picture, that the trauma was now over, and that it had run its course through me. The speculation turned out to be quite premature and completely illusory. What I had not realized was that the deep psychological momentum had not stopped. Of its own volition, the persistent inquiring into self was still going on. Unknown, untouched sensitivities kept surfacing.

Pain

Three weeks after my letter was sent, suddenly, without warning, my limbs and body were aching with a pain so excruciating that to remain still was impossible. Every position I assumed soon became unbearable. I would twist and turn, seeking relief. My body would find a comfortable position and the ache would lessen, then abruptly there it was, flaring in a leg, knee, thigh, shoulder. I would roll over, place my hands to the hurt and agonize. The particular torment would ease, and the muscles begin to relax. For a few minutes, I could rest—then the acute ache would arise in a foot, or along one side. There was no letup, day or night.

On earlier occasions in my life, as when a dentist in Seattle drilled my front teeth without a drug injection, it was a matter of relaxing, watching, feeling, "putting up with it," until the job was done. I knew what was going on, was aware of the source of the pain, and that there would be an end. A relaxed, serene watchfulness permitted me to cope with it.

Now, no real, specific "cause" for my distress had surfaced. I did not know its source, beyond the fact that my self-image had been badly damaged. Though the location of the pain changed, the condition did not. There was no release. For three months, I could not walk or even stand. I crawled whenever I had to move from my bed. I remained in the house, and friends brought me food. The suffering was not continuous but cyclic, coming in waves and subsiding.

Gradually, the self-questioning diminished, but the physical symptoms persisted, endlessly. There was, too, the feeling of being completely alone. I lay watching, experiencing, agonizing. Soon I was no longer interested in understanding, changing, or even getting rid of the dreadful pain. My only concern was with what was actually going on in my body-being. It became obvious that the pain aroused "me" (the feeler of the pain), and when the "me" disappeared so did my awareness of pain; that the observer-experiencer of the agony and the agony arose and waned together as one consciousness. By not trying to be free, by not looking for causes or motives, for answers or ends or for relief, though the pain persisted, my mind was tranquil.

As I lay there I would notice sly wisps of thinking occasionally sliding into consciousness. Once noticed, these thought trails would die away, leaving a kind of extensional awareness, an empty wholeness, until again the ache would start up in some other part of my body. I "knew" there was nothing to be done, that the body-mind-being condition had to run its course. I learned, too, that thought distances itself from pain and then tries to deal with it. My physical condition did not actually alter, even though consciousness did clarify and sharpen.

Where earlier just-below-the-surface fear of the next incursion of pain was ever-waiting, I now had an attentiveness to what was actually *here*. I began to have lengthening periods of unconsciousness. Over the weeks and months the onset of the next bout of pain held less terror and its dominance diminished.

Release

Throughout the travail, there was no feeling of right or wrong, of justice or injustice. What was happening involved senses, consciousness, everything. The whole crisis was real, and somehow completely "right."

I realized that had I been asked for an explanation by Krishnamurti or been given any opportunity to give an account of what had happened, I would have worked at presenting a rationale, a defense. No such chance had been given. I was free to watch what was going on. There was nothing else to do. "I" and "time" had come to a stop. The old impetus, the ongoing process of working in the present for some future result, had dissolved.

I sensed a new freedom. Like a bird that has refused to leave the safety of the nest, I had been nudged out into the air, alone.

Months later I wrote a more sanguine, and perhaps, more apt yet stark metaphor describing my state of mind:

> Unripe fruit clings to the branch
> where it is nurtured and sustained.
> When ripe and ready,
> no longer holding to the bough

and no longer being held
it drops, falls free...
Perhaps to rot on the ground,
Perchance to realize its wholeness,
and burst forth into its own life.

And again:

My life came into crisis.
Suddenly hidden realities
were exposed, opened out,
laid bare....

With this "release" came awareness that it was
not the teachings, seductive though they are, true
though they may be, that had bred my dependen-
cy, but what I had made of them. The teachings
had not freed me; they had, like some superb
mind dynamics course, merely given "the me"
more scope. They had been an overlay, a brilliant
veneer that had obscured direct perception of
what I was and what I was actually doing. It was
not that Krishnamurti had influenced me, but
rather that I had taken from him what I wanted to
enhance my understanding and my life. I had
been on a subtle, semiconscious, partially-under-
stood ego trip. Self-advancement disguised as freedom from self had been my real goal.

I had long since realized that Krishnamurti was
not a computing machine with already stored wisdom and knowledge, giving out answers to whatever questions were put to him. He was a compassionate, awakened human being who opened
out the question, the problem, as it was presented to him. He did not answer questions from
his knowledge but showed the questioner the
makeup of his or her problem, allowing the block-

ages to be seen. He talked to people according to their tendencies and capacity to understand their problem and the problem-maker, themselves.

The teachings stand. Their resonances ring true. Their starkness, intelligence, and seductive beauty are resounding throughout the world. But magnificent as they are, needed as they are, the teachings are not a positive, religious philosophy to be learned and then applied. It was back in 1930, in a talk published under the title "Life's Problems—Introduction," that Krishnamurti said, "You become a light unto yourself and hence you do not cast a shadow across the path of another or the path of yourself." I was casting shadows, and patches of darkness were being reflected back. Working in his light, following his teachings, my "I" could remain hidden and intact. Yet any attempt to live through another's perceptions, however wise, does not free the unique assembly that constitutes "me."

The Krishnamurti work went on, for people wanted to read the books, listen to the tapes, and have discussions. But the enthusiasm, the open, harmonious flow had faltered. The North Sydney and Narrabeen centers closed. Four of those who had willingly accepted responsibility for organizing regular video showings, meetings, and discussions had, on receipt of the letter (mailed directly to each committee member from Madras), decided not to continue.

Three months after it had started, one evening in May, the debilitating pain vanished. It went as suddenly as it had come. Around ten o'clock, without any prior warning, my body felt whole, every particle tinglingly alive with an indescribable sense of vividness. The crisis had passed.

Within a couple of days health picked up, and the mobility and the use of my legs returned. With this renewal came an aloneness and an extraordinary lightness.

A blessing had come.

A Reprieve

Within days of the ending of the pain, another letter from Krishnamurti arrived from Ojai, California, dated April 28, 1983, inviting Mavis Bennett and me to the meeting of the Krishnamurti Foundations from September 7 to 14 at Brockwood.

In this letter he said it was important that we meet to clear up any misunderstanding so that we could all work together amicably. He suggested that funds collected for the work in Australia be used to meet the expenses of the flight to England, and said that room could be found for both of us as guests of Brockwood. "Do please consider both of you coming as I particularly would like to clear up this matter." He asked that this letter be shown to all helpers in Sydney and in other places.

Mavis was not able to make it. I replied that I would be there. As there were no funds, I paid my own fare. Any contributions we received went to buying more books and tapes for distribution, television sets, videotapes, and towards circulating the biannual *Australian Bulletin*. I turned up at Brockwood on August 26.

It so happened that the meeting of the Foundations had been cancelled. An unexpected sum-

mons from California requiring Krishnamurti's
presence in relation to an impending court case
meant that immediately after the Brockwood talks
he had to leave.

The Brockwood Meeting

The next morning I met with Mary Cadogan.*
During the course of the conversation, she wanted
to know how things were in Sydney when I left. I
told her that after the initial shock, disruption,
and resignations, the essential work had gone on,
but that the joy was missing. As months passed
and no replies to the members' letters had come,
the bewilderment had remained and our momentum had faltered. Mary then informed me that
someone from another state in Australia had written a derogatory letter about me, and that this letter, quite apart from the two offending clauses in
the legal document, had been instrumental in
Krishnamurti's writing his letter to me.

It was an intentionally circumspect piece of information, but it cleared up one incomprehensible
factor, something that until then I had known
nothing about. (A month later, in Ojai, I was told
by two members of the American Foundation that
they had read a copy of the disruptive letter,
knew the writer's identity, and understood the letter's implications.) Besides wonder, there came a
sadness that even among those working for free-

---

*Mary Cadogan is the secretary of the English Krish-
namurti Foundation Trust, Ltd.

195

dom in themselves and in the world there could be deliberate destructiveness.

That afternoon I had a session with David Bohm* and Mary. The next day we had another discussion. The talk mainly centered around what procedures were most likely to prove practical in handling the Krishnamurti work in Australia. They wanted to know whether there had been any change in attitude, how our organization was functioning, and what alterations were envisioned. Our conversations were friendly, open, and frank.

What follows is a transcript of my notes, written right after the meeting with Krishnamurti, so that the Australian Committee members would receive the information fresh and clear. I wrote what I was feeling and what had occurred as we talked. (The notes have been slightly edited for readability.)

"Greetings over and once we were seated, Krishnaji asked about the membership and the formation of the Australian Committee. He wanted to know who the members of the new organization were going to be and how we proposed to operate.

"As we talked, I realized that the past was to be forgotten. It was over. A fresh start, free from what had happened, was needed. Good. It was also clear from his questioning that Krishnaji was not interested in the offensive clauses in the

---

*David Bohm is a quantum physicist. Has had over the years numerous dialogues with Krishnamurti, many recorded on audio- and videotapes. Published *Truth and Actuality* and *The Ending of Time*, as well as *Wholeness and The Implicate Order.*

Memorandum and Articles of Association, nor in
the legal problems, nor his letters to me (they
were never mentioned). His concern seemed to be
exclusively with the selection of those persons
who would be invited to form a single nationwide
committee.

"It was proposed that there be two representatives from each of the seven Australian states.*
Krishnamurti asked what could be done in this regard. I said I felt that such an arrangement would
be impractical. In a continent approximately the
same area as the United States and far bigger than
Europe, distance and cost would make communication difficult, operation laborious, and even annual meetings virtually impossible.

"Krishnaji listened without comment. He clearly had reservations about setting up a national organization, and perhaps had doubts about any
closely related local committee."

This surmise was confirmed when a list of suit-
able persons to serve on the Australian committee
was produced. We went through the names one
by one. They included not only those who were
regarded as acceptable, but those who were to be
omitted, based, as I was told, on the tenor of the
letters they had written to Krishnaji.

That a list was being compiled in England of
those who were to be asked to operate in Australia
disturbed me. There were to be checks, and,
though benign, an external authority was being
set up. Of course, the functioning of any
worldwide movement presents problems. By permitting groups to develop along their own lines,

----

*There are six Australian states plus the Northern Ter-
ritory (the seventh state).

there is the ever-present possibility, even likelihood, of division and disruption, and of the rise of interpreters and factions. And so, inevitably, centralized structures have been the method of control throughout history. This practice persists even though remote authoritative control can exacerbate the problems inherent in local operations.

Since power corrupts, is there anything that can be done organizationally to free humans from self-bondage? Here I had a delicious realization. What I was objecting to—supervision from London or Brockwood or Ojai or Adyar or anywhere else— was in no real way different from the proposal of a group based in Sydney, which COULD assume control of Krishnamurti's activities in Australia, and thus perpetuate a similar hierarchical structure with all its possibilities for division.

Krishnaji then asked, "Is there anything further to be discussed, something you want to bring up?" Yes, there was. I asked if there was any need for those who had received his original letter to be told that I was no longer persona non grata. Krishnaji's reply, "You tell them, sir," was direct and unequivocal. He was once again turning me around, allowing me to see that the decision for whatever I might do was mine, and with it the responsibility.

Right then I realized there was no problem, none at all. There could be one only if I were to make this into a "situation to be resolved." Any difficulty that arose would be of my own making. Krishnaji was free. And, in letting go, so was I.

We sat quietly for a few moments. Then Krishnaji asked again, "Is there anything more?" The meeting was over. I walked to my room in the cloisters.

Even though nothing had been resolved with regard to the work in Australia or my function in it, a great deal had happened. Besides a real apprehension concerning the free, open, and successful functioning of any worldwide organization that may be envisioned, there was an enormous sense of aloneness.

Mark Edwards

A Beginning

Consequences

There was no question then or now as to whether to carry on with the Krishnamurti work. I saw no intrinsic difference between acting with others in the world and learning about myself; between Krishnamurti's insights into the human condition and my own quest for self-understanding. Together they constituted a complementary inward-outward interaction. Once the yeast of inquiry had begun, I really had no choice. The thrill of living, of the beauty of the earth and sky, of following thoughts and feelings were my deep and profound joy.

However, at unexpected moments, contending sensations like so many demons would invade consciousness. Clearly, so long as any agitating memories of what had occurred continued to surface, they had to be traced to their still-present source; otherwise the new-found freedom was fragile and could vanish at any time. An incident could reactivate whatever residue remained unresolved. So what was still hidden and needing to be uncovered and seen? I had to go after it and bring it to light. Months later I was able to write about it.

In retrospect, it now seems unlikely that those apparently rather small incidents should have trig-

gered such a profound storm in my body-being.
Why had this been such a catalyst for me? After
all, I had talked and probed and been exposed in
many different ways by Krishnaji on many earlier
occasions.

The fact is that I still really do not know. I surmise that the revolutionary germ-seed of a new dimension emerges out of the old in one whole
movement. For when the psychological ego
trauma had passed, so had the stress and anguish.
The excruciating pain, physical and mental,
which at the time had seemed unbearable, had
gone, leaving little trace. And what did linger for
eighteen months or so gradually disappeared until
it now seems as though it had never been.

I ask myself: If all the hurt has actually gone
why am I writing about it? Why this consequence? Probably I'm writing because the crisis
was an integral part of the whole experience.
Somehow, and it does not now really matter what
triggered it, a critical tension or focusing of
energy had occurred, forcing a breakdown of self
or a breakthrough into self.

To what extent the entrenched entity "me" released itself, I do not know. Yet without the catalyst of Krishnamurti's calling halt to my activities, it is unlikely that any real change in my life
pattern would have happened. Any attempt now
to recapture what happened would be illusory, as
would any speculation as to what, if anything,
had been in Krishnamurti's mind.

It was not Krishnamurti who had pressured me
into whatever predicament I found myself in.
What I encountered then, or experience anytime,
is always of my own making.

There is an enormous gratefulness to Krishnaji

for being, for the teachings, and for so profoundly shaking the very foundations of my being. As it turned out, I really had nothing to do about my reinstatement. I only had to go on doing the work. As Krishnaji said, "It's up to you."

There was, however, the matter of the spreading of the revolutionary self-revealing message. Here is Krishnamurti's answer given to that question when it was put to him in Madras in 1947. A man asked: "I am very interested in your teachings; I would like to spread them. What is the best way to do it?"

Krishnamurti: "Many things are involved in this question. Let us look at it. Propaganda is a lie because mere repetition is not truth. What you can repeat is a lie. Truth cannot be repeated, for truth can only be experienced directly; mere repetition is a lie because repetition implies imitation. That which you repeat may be truth to someone, but when you repeat it, it ceases to be truth. Propaganda is one of the terrible things in which we are caught. You know something or you don't know. Usually you have read something in some books and you have heard some talk and you want to spread it. Have words any significance besides the verbal meaning? So what you are spreading is really words, and do words or terms resolve our problems? Say, for instance, you believe in reincarnation; you don't know why you believe, but you want to spread that belief. What are you spreading in fact? Your belief, terms, words; your convictions which are still within the field, within the layer of verbal expression.

"We think in words, in terms; we seek explanations which are still only words, and we are caught in this monstrous lie, believing that the word is the thing. Surely, the word 'God' is not God, but you believe that the word is God and that therefore you can spread it. Please see this. To you, the *word* has become important, and not reality. So you are caught in the verbal level, and what you want to spread is the word. That means you will catch what I am saying in the net of words and so cause a new division between man and man. Then you will create a new system based on Krishnamurti's words, which you the propagandist will spread among other propagandists who are also caught in words—and thereby what have you done? Whom have you helped? No, sirs, that is not the way to spread. So don't try what is stupid, what is the height of folly—to spread someone else's experience.

"If you experience something directly, it would be experience not based on belief, because what you believe, you experience; and therefore it is not real experience but only conditioned experience. There can be experience, the right kind of experience, only when thinking ceases, but that experience cannot be spread as information to clear the mess. But if you begin to understand simple things like nationalism, surely you can discuss it with others, in order to make it known as a poison which is destroying man. Sirs, you are not aware of the enormous calamity that lies in wait for you and for the whole world because this poison is spreading. You are nationalists, you are Hindus, against Pakistan, against England, against Germany, against Russia, and so on. So, nationalism is a poison, is it not? You can understand that very easily because it divides men. You cannot be a nationalist and talk of brotherhood; these terms are contradictory.

"That also you can understand, that you can

talk about. But you don't want to talk about that because that would mean a change of heart within yourself, which means that you must cease to be a Hindu, with your beliefs, ceremonies, and all the rubbish that is around you. We don't talk about nationalism because we might be asked if we are free of it ourselves. Not being free, we evade it, and try to discuss something else. Surely you can talk about something which you live and which you are doing every day, and that is what I have been talking about—your daily actions, your daily thoughts, and feelings. My words you cannot repeat, for, if you do, they will have no meaning; but you can talk about the way you live, the way you act, the way you think, from which alone there can be understanding; all that, you can discuss; but there is no use of groups with presidents and secretaries and organizations, which are terrible things in which you are often caught. Sirs, though you all smile, yet surely you are all caught in these. I don't think you know how catastrophic the whole situation is in the world now. I don't have to frighten you. You have merely to pick up a newspaper and read about it. You are on the edge of a precipice and you still perform ceremonies, carry on in your stupid ways, blind to what is happening. You can only alter by transformation of yourself and not by the introduction of a new system, whether of the left or of the right. In the transformation of yourself is the only hope, but you cannot transform yourself, radically, profoundly, if you are above all a Hindu, if you perform ceremonies, if you are caught in the net of organizations.

"As it has always been in the past, so also at the present time the salvation of man is in his being creative. You are caught inwardly in belief, in fear, and in those hindrances that prevent the coming together of mind and man. That is, if I don't know how to love you, how to love my neighbor, my wife, how can there be communion between us? We need communion; not communion between systems, but communion between you and me without systems, without organizations, and that means we must really know how to love one another. Our hearts must be opened to one another, but your hearts cannot be open if you belong to an organization, if you are bound by beliefs, if you are nationalistic, if you are a Brahmin or a Sudra [castes]. So, you can spread even a tiny part of what I have been talking about only as you live. It is by your life that you communicate profoundly, not through words. Words, sirs, to a serious, thoughtful man have very little meaning. Terms are of very little significance when you are really seeking truth, truth in relationship and not an abstract truth of valuations, of things, or of ideas. If you want to find the truth of those things verbally, it is of little importance; but words become very important when you are not seeking truth; then the word is the thing and the thing catches you. So, if you want to spread these teachings, live them, and by your life you will be spreading them. You will be communicating them, which is much more true and significant than verbal repetition, for repetition is imitation and imitation is not creativeness, and you as an individual must awake to your own conditioning and thereby free yourself and hence give love to another."

For such a metamorphosis there is only one starting point, and that is with me, here and now, in daily living and relationships.

Teacher as Mirror

No teacher produces another like himself. In life there is no exact repetition. In nature no two waves roll onto a beach in the same way, no two days or seasons replicate each other. Any attempt to imitate Krishnamurti is unrealistic. Even so, listening to his superb descriptions of consciousness, I would experience an aliveness and a sense of freedom, and I would want "more." This set up an impossible dichotomy; a greed to store what I had heard and an awareness that the very act of listening dissolved normal consciousness. In reality there is nothing to remember. As when a pain has passed from the body, why keep it going in thought? When an old hurt has healed and the present is free, why hold the pain in memory? Even so, the unseen, unresolved residuals soon reestablish their old domain.

One early morning, as I lay in bed in that state between waking and sleeping, it came to me that the brain is like a subtle, psychological spider's web. Touch it and the whole microscopic matrix vibrates. Hit it and the web bounces back. Such resilience ensures the continuity of the established mode. Sometimes a thread breaks and before the spider can mend its web—or before I myself can reinstate the old thought pattern—a space appears

briefly. In those few seconds and through that
gap, another reality can enter which then becomes
part of my thought web.

In such a metaphorical manner had Krishnamurti's devastating insights entered my consciousness. Pointing up my reluctance to foresake his
perceptions is the fact that I sometimes catch
myself using his very words as though they were
my own observations, phrases like: to be is to be
related; the thinker and the thought are one; the
observer is the observed; consciousness is its content; freedom is freedom from the known; what
is—is sacred; the description is not the described;
you and the world are one.

Krishnamurti's passionate penetration into the
human psyche and consciousness rings so true,
has such immediate clarity, that my unwillingness
to relinquish his insights as touchstones for my
own observations persisted even after I had
worked through the hidden realities in myself. For
thirty-five years I had been attempting the un-
real—to function in and through Krishnamurti's
mind while living within my own construction of
reality. An impossible feat.

Still, it is so much easier to repeat remembered
truths (Krishnamurti's, my own, or anyone's) than
it is to do the arduous work of uncovering my
present consciousness. I had remained a follower,
meanwhile neglecting to observe with similar zeal
and attention what was going on in me. In so doing I had been overlooking some important factors
in the teacher-pupil relationship. For example, by
trying to understand Krishnamurti's insights, I
had missed the bare fact that in making his perceptions (or my understanding of his perceptions)

into masks and wearing them over mine, I could remain in hiding and survive.

My misconception had been in viewing Krishnamurti primarily as the teacher and not as a mirror.

Listening. Just Listening

I have had it wrong all my life. I've been looking
for improvement, change for the better. Whenever
I noticed something painful, foolish or false I
worked at ways to improve the situation or to
change myself. At four o'clock one morning I
awoke and knew that this process, acceptable in
the physical world, is utterly meaningless in the
inner world.

What I actually saw was: Stop whatever I am
doing the moment I am aware that it is not true.
That is all. No positive action whatsoever.

The implications are vast. First, the negation of
the false is wholly positive because it is immediately finished, there and then. No time is needed
to correct the error. There is no changing this for
that; no thought for the future that "I will not
make this mistake again."

While the unwanted is held in mind so that it
can be seen, understood and hopefully resolved,
the problem is being sustained. To try to stop
thinking about something is impossible because I
have to keep it in mind in order to remember not
to think about it, and thereby keeping alive what I
want to forget. Clearly the critical point is the moment I am aware there is a disturbance. For example, the instant I sense I am overeating, to stop.

Of if I catch myself exaggerating or lying, to pause and listen. On noticing anger rising, to wait and watch. Perception alone dictating, directing, letting go.

Given no energy, the false atrophies. Living takes on a new freedom. I find myself listening, not to outside noises or for guidance, nor to inward thoughts and feelings. Just listening. Not to learn about myself and life gradually, through time, at my convenience. Listening. Just listening.

When the Teacher Dies

It was my great good fortune to have on occasion been close to Krishnamurti. And now he is dead. Perhaps for the first time in human history the complete teachings of a world teacher are on record. His writings, books, tapes, and the verbatim reports of thousands of talks, discussions, and dialogues are there for everyone, open to all. Faulty memories, misrepresentations, and misinterpretations have no place in and cannot warp "the teaching," for everyone can go directly to the source.

As always when the teacher dies, the teachings become the teacher. Throughout historical time this phenomenon has occurred. Learning from the great and the wise has been recognized as humanity's passport to progress, its "onward and upward" advance. Each succeeding civilization has its roots in what has previously been discovered and found to work, and in the unquestioned belief in the ascent of man.

However, when spiritual, ethical, philosophical, and cultural mores are examined critically, the "teacher-teaching-student-learning" sequence exposes a totally contrary reality. Psychically, inwardly, the transforming teachings have not helped humanity. Indeed, they have been a hindrance. Learning what the sages and enlightened ones have said (and written) about the "other" dimension has failed. Fear, hate, anger, jealousy, egotism, violence, aggression, and war are everywhere present, perhaps even on the increase.

Clearly, reality, awareness, inward freedom is not something that can be taught by one and learned by another, nor can it be imitated. Unravelling "self" is the task, the responsibility, and the joy of each individual.

The following selections are taken from Krishnamurti's recorded talks and discussions across the world:

"You have to be your own teacher and your own disciple, and there is no teacher outside, no savior, no master; you yourself have to change and, therefore, you have to learn to observe, to know yourself. This learning about yourself is a fascinating and joyous business."

Talks with American Students, Berkeley: Shambhala Publications, 1970

"One has to find out for oneself. . . This doesn't mean that you reject what others say but that you enquire without acceptance or denial. An aggressive mind, a mind tethered to a belief, is not free and therefore it is incapable of enquiry. All this demands intensive enquiry, not acceptance."

Talks and Discussions at Brockwood Park, Berkeley: Shambhala Publications, 1970, pp. 38-39

"Can anyone teach you that extraordinary state of mind? They may be able to describe it to you, awaken your interest, your desire to possess it, experience it—but they cannot give it to you. You have to walk by yourself, you have to take the journey alone, and on that journey you have to be your own teacher and pupil."

The Only Revolution, Mary Lutyens, ed., New York and Evanston: Harper & Row, 1970, p. 38

"What you learn from another is not true. So you have to find out for yourself what you are and to learn how to observe yourself."

Krishnamurti in India, 1970-71, Krishnamurti Foundation, India, 1971, p. 84

"Nobody can give guidance, can give light, to another. Only you yourself can do that; but you have to stand completely alone. That is what is frightening for the old and the young. If you belong to anything, follow anybody, you are already entering into corruption."

Questions and Answers, Krishnamurti Trust Ltd., England, 1982, p. 47-49

Having once realized that the gateway is myself, the journey through self takes on another meaning—and other profound crises.

There is no prelearned approach to a crisis, for it is totally unpredictable. I am either taken completely by surprise, or my known resources have failed to meet the challenge. It is the critical breakdown or breakthrough point when the past actually, for the moment, ends. Crisis is, in fact, the gateway to an unknown dimension, an ever-new reality.

Again Krishnamurti: "Reality is a peculiar thing. Reality is a living thing and cannot be captured and you cannot say it is always there. There is a path only to something which is stationary, to a fixed, static point. To a living thing which is constantly in movement, which has no resting place, how can there be a guide, a path? Can you put aside the teacher, the path, the end—put it aside so completely that your mind is empty of all this seeking?

"To be quiet requires great energy; you need all your energy for silence of the mind and it is only in emptiness, in complete emptiness, that a new thing can be."

Eight Conversations, Krishnamurti
Foundation, London, 1969, p. 4

Not Knowing

After all the trauma, the searching and effort of learning through another, I'm back to me. There really is nothing to be done but to live and observe the responses that are my consciousness; to be aware of the reflections in my mind. I am one example of those who did not hear or see the basic truth at the very core of "the teachings." Do not learn from me. Learn about yourself from yourself. Certainly Krishnamurti is the one teacher who refuses to be a leader and who turns the pupil back onto himself.

At the grave risk of appearing to trivialize the wondrous journey with Krishnamurti, it is true to say that it was like at the end of *The Wizard of Oz* when the Good Witch tells Dorothy, "You had the power to go home all along." Dorothy cries out, "Why didn't you tell me, before I had to go through all this?" And the Good Witch replies, "Because you wouldn't have believed me."

All along I had been one who did not clearly hear the essential message that liberation—enlightenment, freedom, by whatever name—is an ending of self and is not an ego achievement, and so "I" cannot learn it or use it. The fact is that for fifty years and more Krishnamurti had been saying to anyone awake enough to hear him, "It is very important not to follow anyone, including the speaker,'' and, ''You are the teacher, the taught and the teaching.''

My daily round is fairly routine, thinking out things to do and doing them, and rediscovering in the process that every act produces another set of circumstances to be lived through, other problems to be solved. And, in the meantime, the problem-maker/problem-solver persists, or more accurately, the ''me'' reemerges.

At other times (as happened a few mornings ago) the old question of what to do returns. Is there anything to be done? Anything I can do? I put it directly to myself—aloud:

        What...can...I...do?

I listened. No answer.

I waited. Nothing came...nothing. The emptiness remained.

Then, in the silence, quite suddenly, came the realization that the wholeness I had been seeking (and not finding) was present—not ''out there'' in time and space, not somewhere else, but intrinsically here and now. Silence danced through me. I saw that when the brain/mind stops churning and is still, the longed-for blissful dimension is already here.

It was starkly obvious that as long as the seeker goes on seeking, the searcher, ''myself,'' will persist. And further, that the seeker *is* the sought, for the sought is the projection of the seeker. What I had been seeking was the seeker, the ''me.'' All this was seen because consciousness was not occupied. That was all. A thrilling aliveness had become a dynamic emptiness that is not void— space filled with energy.

Suddenly, as I sat there, inner space and space

outside interflowed, were indivisibly one.

Later I was aware that each breath, every inhalation and outflow, is reestablishing the timeless communion.

QUEST BOOKS
are published by
The Theosophical Society in America,
Wheaton, Illinois 60189-0270,
a branch of a world organization
dedicated to the promotion of brotherhood and
the encouragement of the study of religion,
philosophy, and science, to the end that man may
better understand himself and his place in
the universe. The Society stands for complete
freedom of individual search and belief.
In the Classics Series well-known
theosophical works are made
available in popular editions.

Quest
Books

We publish books on:
Healing and Health ● Metaphysics and
Mysticism ● Transpersonal Psychology
Philosophy ● Religion ● Reincarnation,
Science ● Yoga and Meditation.
Other books of possible interest include:

At the Feet of the Master *by "Alcyone"*
Krishnamurti's precepts for right living

Beyond Individualism *by Dane Rudhyar*
From ego-centeredness to higher consciousness

Cayce, Karma and Reincarnation *by I. C. Sharma*
Similarity between philosophies of Cayce and India

The Choicemaker *by E. Howes & S. Moon*
Our need to make choices as vital to our evolution

Commentaries on Living *by J. Krishnamurti*
Series 1, 2 & 3. Dialogue on many aspects of living

A Great Awakening *by Robert Powell*
Comparison of Krishnamurti and Zen philosophies

Opening of the Wisdom Eye *by Dalai Lama*
The path of enlightenment through Buddhism

A Way to Self Discovery *by I. K. Taimni*
Way of life for serious aspirants of esoteric wisdom

Whispers from the Other Shore *by Ravi Ravindra*
How religion helps us search for the center of being

Wisdom, Bliss & Common Sense *by Darshani Deane*
Distills arcane secrets of self-transformation

Available from:
The Theosophical Publishing House
P. O. Box 270, Wheaton, Illinois 60189-0270